A CONTEMPORARY STUDY OF THE
HOLY SPIRIT

CHURCH TRAINING COURSE 305

Prepared under the auspices of the Church of God
General Sunday School and Youth Board

A
Contemporary Study of the HOLY SPIRIT

BENNIE S. TRIPLETT

PATHWAY PRESS   Cleveland, Tennessee

DEDICATION

A *Contemporary Study of the Holy Spirit* is gratefully dedicated to the Church of God Home for Children which provided me a home at the age of ten and in a sense demonstrated Christ's words, "I will not leave you orphans . . . I will come . . . to you" (John 14:18, *Amplified New Testament.*)

FOREWORD

I am happy to have the privilege to write the foreword to this book for two specific reasons. One reason is that the book is a very special book, and the other reason is that the author is a special person.

First, about the author. Bennie S. Triplett is a living example of the marvelous grace of God. Orphaned at an early age he was placed in the Church of God Home for Children. The investment the church made in this young child was to prove to be one of its wisest investments. While still in his teen years, he received a call to the Christian ministry. He began an evangelistic singing ministry and was soon conducting revival meetings doing both the singing and preaching. In 1948 he was married to Helen Williams, who has been a faithful companion and Christian helper, as well as devoted mother of their two fine children, Rene and Steve. Bennie has served the Church of God as pastor, Program Director for the general radio program, State Sunday School and Youth Director, General Evangelism Board member, and State Overseer.

One of the prominent aspects of his current ministry is that of a most excellent Bible teacher. And this brings me to my second reason for being pleased to write this foreword, for this book contains a most enlightening Bible study—A Contemporary Study of the Holy Spirit. There exists today a great need for Christians to understand the person and work of the Holy Spirit. This study presents scripturally documented facts that will both inform and inspire the student. This is a very special book since it is the first in the Church Training Program that deals with the doctrine of the Holy Spirit.

This Church Training Course was submitted to the

Executive Council of the Church of God and was approved and endorsed by the council in the May 1970 meeting.

I commend the author and pray that the Holy Spirit will anoint the ministry of this book.

Paul F. Henson

INTRODUCTION

To be contemporary is to be with the times. Britain's Dr. Norman Maclean tells of a parish schoolteacher who required the class to memorize the Apostle's Creed and repeat it clause by clause with each pupil having his own clause. The recitation began with the first boy quoting, "I believe in God the Father Almighty, Maker of heaven and earth." The recitation continued through the words of the boy who said, "from thence He shall come to judge the quick and the dead." Suddenly there fell a silence that indicated something had gone wrong. The silence was broken by the next boy in the line who informed his teacher, "Please sir, the boy who believes in the Holy Ghost is absent today." On which Dr. Maclean commented, "Lots of folks are absent when it comes to that clause."

Admittedly the subject of the Holy Spirit was once referred to as "the forgotten doctrine of the church." Some described it as the most central and the most neglected of the Christian faith. Many were known to have emphasized every other doctrine except the Holy Spirit. For others this was an unspeakably tender subject which often raised defense barriers, thus closing minds and hearts to a most important concern. It is heartening, however, to note that a revival of interest has broken through in our time. Millions are expressing hunger for spiritual food to feed their inner souls. They crave a reality that is more than things. The void is for the spiritual, for they seek and need God.

With much appreciation, acknowledgment is made of the great emphasis which my church has placed on the ministry of the Holy Spirit in the life of the individual and in the life of the church. The commissioning of this book to be placed within one of its primary training agencies is an example of such. May this interest and emphasis never wane. Acknowledgment is therefore given to the leaders and board of the General Sunday School and Youth Department, to the numerous readers who gave counsel and instruction, to the authors and publishers for permission to quote from their works, as well as apologies to any who were overlooked. A deep debt of gratitude is expressed to General Director, Paul F. Henson; also to the Executive Council of the Church of God and its review committee, Rev. Wade H. Horton, Dr. James A. Cross and Rev. Cecil B. Knight. A very special tribute must go to my dear wife, Helen, who typed and read the manuscript again and again; also to our daughter, René, and our son, Steve, for their patience in taking more than their share of the work load around our home.

One never feels more inadequate than when trying to instruct others. Divine guidance is especially needed when one undertakes to give instructions concerning the Holy Spirit. Fully aware of its imperfections, this work is therefore committed to the use and proclamation of that blessed Person of whom it speaks, with the prayer that the Spirit Himself might indeed teach us concerning Himself.

THE CHURCH TRAINING COURSE SERIES

A Contemporary Study of the Holy Spirit is written by Bennie S. Triplett and is one of the study books in the special study course (CTC 305). A "Certificate of Credit" is awarded on the basis of the following requirements:

I. The written review and instructions for preparing the review are listed on page 142. The written review must be completed, reviewed by the pastor or someone whom he may designate, and the name of the student sent to the state office. (No grade will be given for the written review.)

II. The book must be read through.

III. Training sessions must be attended unless permission for absence is granted by the instructor.

IV. The written review is not an examination, but is designated to review the text and reinforce the information presented in the text. Students should research the text for the proper answers.

V. Church Training Course credit may be secured by home study, if no classes are conducted in this course of study.

A training record should be kept in the local church for each person who studies this and other courses in the Church Training Course program. A record form, CTC 33, will be furnished upon request from the state office.

TABLE OF CONTENTS

Introduction --- 9

Foreword --- 11

1. THE HOLY SPIRIT IN DEFINITION ---- 15

2. THE HOLY SPIRIT IN EXPERIENCE 45

3. THE HOLY SPIRIT IN
   DEMONSTRATION ------------------------------- 73

4. THE HOLY SPIRIT IN
   MANIFESTATION ------------------------------- 89

5 THE HOLY SPIRIT AND THE
   CONTEMPORARY SCENE ------------------- 111

6. THE HOLY SPIRIT IN YOU
   (Conclusion) --- 139

1

The Holy Spirit in Definition

"What Meaneth This"

What do we mean when we say "Holy Spirit," "Glossolalia Phenomenon," "Holy Ghost," "Charismatic Endowment," or use the term "Pentecostal"? To define the terms which we use is the aim of the opening chapter of this book.

Words and meanings often change. Language is sometimes subject to rapid change. Almost every age, culture or discipline demands and usually produces its own vocabulary. Thomas Aquinas recognized such a problem in his day and endeavored to fuse the terms of philosophy and theology. Even in our time we are witnessing a synthesis of the semantics of psychology and theology.

It is important that we define or state specifically the meaning of the basic language which we will use. If we are to conduct a contemporary study, we need to know what certain key words mean and how they will be used. Therefore, we will attempt to define the primary language related to a study of the Holy Spirit.

"Holy"

The word "holy" is used in the Scriptures to refer to persons and things which are sacred and set apart for holy uses. When it applies to God, it signifies His separation from and His transcendency over all His creation. It refers to His majesty and supremacy, as well as the ethical spotlessness of His character (Lev. 11:44; 1 Peter 1:16). When applied to objects and institutions, it is not that they are "holy" in themselves, but that their uses are withdrawn from common employment and dedicated to God's service.[1] In the Old Testament the Hebrew word *qadosh* renders the word "holy" to designate heavenly beings such as angels and deities; and the word "saints" to denote mortals of high spiritual worth.

In the New Testament, the Greek word *hagios* is used of things, men, angels and God. It refers to that which is consecrated or devoted to a deity.[2] A. J. Gordon declares "Christlikeness" to be synonymous with "holiness." It is the work of the Spirit to minister "Christ" to and through the church. The exercise of love is the "means" which God uses to develop Christlikeness in His children. In the strictest sense, God is the only absolute Holy One.[3] The essential nature of the Godhead is holiness. Because the Spirit is indeed God, the term "Holy" is appropriately used. To use the term in referring to mortal man or to things, is not to speak of qualities of their making, but qualities and attributes which reflect Godlikeness or Christlikeness. Ours, then becomes a sun and

---

1 Paul S. Rees, *Baker's Dictionary of Theology*, Baker Book House, Grand Rapids, 1960, pp. 269, 270.

2 Alan Richardson, *Theological Word Book*, MacMillan Co., New York, 1950, p. 215.

3 W. E. Vine, *Expository Dictionary*, Fleming H. Revell Co., 1969, pp. 26, 27.

moon relationship, the moon having no source of light within itself, but only reflecting the true source.

But why the use of the prefixed word "Holy" with the Spirit, when the adjective is only used sparingly with the Father and the Son? Myer Pearlman says, "The Spirit is called 'Holy' because He is the Spirit of the Holy One, and His chief work is sanctification."[4]

Bancroft says,

> The essential moral character of the Spirit is emphasized by this name. He is Holy in person and character; and is also the director of holiness in men. The Spirit is not called "Holy" with more frequency than the other persons of the Trinity because He is more holy, for infinite holiness does not admit degrees. He is thus officially designated because it is His work to make holy.[5]

J. M. Pendleton states,

> The Spirit is emphatically called "Holy" to denote official distinction. He is termed "Holy" because it is His office to make holy. It is His work to deposit the germ of holiness in the sinful heart of man. There is no holiness in any human heart till the Holy Spirit produces it. The Third Person in the Godhead is designated "the Holy Spirit" because He renovates the soul, purifies it and prepares it for heaven.[6]

As the "Holy Spirit" so designated, is it not significant that every kind of sin and blasphemy can be forgiven except one, and that is against the Holy Ghost (Matt. 12:31, 32; Mark 3:28, 29; Luke 12:10)? Is it not also

---

4 Myer Pearlman, *Knowing the Doctrines of the Bible*, Gospel Pub. House, Springfield, Mo., 1937, p. 287. Used by permission.

5 Emery H. Bancroft, *Elemental Theology*, Zondervan Pub. House, Grand Rapids, 1963, p. 160.

6 J. M. Pendleton, *Christian Doctrines*, Judson Press, Chicago, 1964, p. 95. Used by permission.

significant that it is a dangerous thing "to lie" to or "to tempt" the Holy Spirit (Acts 5:3, 9)?

"Spirit"

What shall we say concerning the Spirit, except that He is Holy and He is God. According to Dr. Alan Richardson the word almost defies analysis.

There is but one Hebrew word (ruah) and one Greek word (pneuma) for "spirit" as understood in the sense of the incorporeal aspect of human nature. The Old Testament word for "spirit" is also rendered pneuma in the LXX (Septuagint).[7] The Old Testament stresses the Spirit's activity in man, and His activity in sustaining that which has been created (Gen. 1:2; Job 26:13; Psa. 104:30; Job 34:14).

The Greek word for "spirit" in the New Testament is pneuma, which corresponds to the Hebrew ruach. Both words seem to refer to an "invisible force." Here the emphasis is also on the Spirit's activity. Pneuma primarily denotes the "wind" and "breath," which is invisible, immaterial and powerful.[8] Wind refers to that beneficient or destructive invisible instrument of the equally unseen God. Breath refers to that "vital stuff" created by God and imparted as life to man (Gen. 2:7). "Spirit" carries with it God's dynamic, creative and sustaining activity; for if God should take back His Spirit, all flesh would perish (Job 34:14; Psa. 104:29, 30). This inward invisible force is God's direct touch, by which all things are upheld and all creatures receive a vital, necessary life from God. The Holy Spirit, then, is the Person in the Holy Trinity whose office work it is to sustain

---

7 The Pre-Christian Greek Version of the (Hebrew) Old Testament.
8 Vine, op. cit., p. 82.

the life principle of God in every creature, animate every rational being, and dwell in the hearts of the elect.[9]

"Ghost"

The Holy Spirit is spoken of under various titles in the New Testament. "Spirit" and "Ghost" are two renderings of the same Greek word *pneuma*. The advantage of the rendering "Spirit" is that it can always be used, whereas, "Ghost" requires the word "Holy" to be prefixed.[10] The English word "ghost" is from the Anglo-Saxon *gast* or *gest*, meaning an inmate, inhabitant or guest. The word "spirit" in its restricted meaning refers to the immortal soul and spirit of man, the guest or indweller of the body. In German, the word *geist* is also used with its connotation of "guest."

In certain areas, the term "Holy Spirit" is thought to be more proper than the term "Holy Ghost." There is really no difference in the meaning, as both terms are synonymous. When the two terms are used in the New Testament, they are two different translations of the same original word and have the same meaning. The probable reason for the King James Version translators using the two titles interchangeably was to connote the idea represented in the Anglo-Saxon and German derivities of *gast* and *geist* meaning "guest."

A guest is a person entertained in one's house, a person to whom the hospitality of a home is extended and refers to any person who lodges there, or has been received there. The Holy Ghost, then, is not only a gift of God, but He is also a Divine Guest from God who

---

9 Abraham Kuyper, *The Work of the Holy Spirit*, Wm. B. Eerdmans Pub. Co., Grand Rapids, 1900, p. 26.
10 Vine, *op. cit.*, Vol. IV. p. 63.

dwells *with* and *in* (John 14:17; 1 Cor. 3:16) the human heart.

"Third Person of the Trinity"

The Holy Spirit is the Third Person of the Trinity. The second article in the Church of God Declaration of Faith states, "We believe . . . In one God eternally existing in three persons; namely, the Father, Son, and Holy Ghost." The tenth article declares, "We believe . . . In water baptism by immersion, and all who repent should be baptized in the name of the Father, and of the Son, and of the Holy Ghost."[11] Thus, the true formula for water baptism as authorized by our Lord, lists the members of the Trinity in an order that designates the Holy Spirit as the Third Person (Matt. 28:19). This listing and order of the Godhead is further validated by the Scripture, "For there are three that bear record in heaven, the Father, the Word, and the Holy Ghost: and these three are one" (1 John 5:7).

But you ask, how can three persons be one? The only sense in which three can be one is in "unity" as is clear in numerous Scriptures. (See Gen. 2:24, 11:6; John 17:11, 21-23; 1 Cor. 3:6-8, 12:13; Eph. 2:14; Heb. 2:11.) "One in unity" means union with and consecrated to the same end—one mind, one purpose and life.

> The word *Trinity* or tri-unity refers to the one being of God as Father, Son and Holy Spirit. This doctrine has been the primary and distinctive Christian conception of God since the early centuries of the Church. It is also a central mystery of the Christian Faith and the most difficult to state adequately. The revela-

---

11 1968 *Minutes of the Fifty-Second General Assembly of the Church of God*, Supplement, p. 4.

tion or disclosure of God as Father, Son and the Holy Spirit is not simply a human view of ways in which God is related to the world, but is God Himself relating to the world. It is His "ways of being God," thus the mystery of divine life.[12]

Alan Richardson explains,

The word *Trinity* is not found in the Scriptures but its threefold doxological and liturgical formulae (e.g. Matt. 28:19; 2 Cor. 1:21f., 13:14; 1 Peter 1:2; Jude 20ff.; Rev. 1:4-6) sufficiently demonstrates that the apostolic church worshiped one God in Trinity and Trinity in unity. . . .[13]

I should not proceed without offering the caution of James L. Slay, who says,

The first great schism in the modern Pentecostal churches took place because of the so-called New Light —New Issue—"Jesus Only" Doctrine, those who baptize in "Jesus name" and feel that a person is not really converted unless one believes as they do and are baptized as they are.[14]

To this I would add that the contemporary look of some of these groups has changed. In many instances their name is no longer "Jesus Only," and they seldom mention their doctrine unless confronted. Their emphasis is on "Pentecost," "The baptism of the Holy Ghost" and "speaking in tongues," yet their doctrine denies the Trinity and embraces the "Jesus Only—Oneness" concept. These denominations and groups are not members and cannot become members of the World Pentecostal Fel-

---

[12] *Handbook of Christian Theology*, World Pub. Co., Cleveland, Ohio, 1958, pp. 366, 368.

[13] Alan Richardson, *An Introduction to the Theology of the New Testament.* Harper & Row, 1958, p. 122.

[14] James L. Slay, *This We Believe*, Pathway Press, Cleveland, Tenn., 1963, pp. 27, 28.

lowship, the Pentecostal Fellowship of North American or the National Association of Evangelicals so long as they embrace their erroneous concept. This is another reason the student of the Word should study the Scriptural concept of the Trinity[15] The term *Trinity* is further explained by the word "triune." It is a compound of the words *tri* meaning "three" and the Latin word *unus* meaning "one," thus meaning "three in one."[16] The word *Trinity* means the union of three persons (the Father, the Son, and the Holy Ghost) in one Godhead, so that all the three are one God as to substance, but three Persons as to individuality.[17]

The term "third" has no relationship to rank, authority or power, but is used as a simple numerical convenience in listing the scriptural and traditional formula. It is not used in the sense of subordination, even though numerous scriptures refer to the Godhead relationship. (See John 6:38, 13:16, 14:28, 17:7; Rom. 2:16, 3:22, 5:1, 11, 17, 21; 1 Cor. 3:23; Eph. 1:5; 1 Thess. 5:9; Titus 3:5.) It is used only as the logical and liturgical sequence given in the baptismal and benedictional formulas. The Three are equal. There is no difference in glory, power or length of existence. The listing of the Holy Spirit after the Father and the Son is simply one of order.[18]

The term *Third Person* of the Trinity means that the Holy Spirit is a Person. Thiessen gives a concise treatment in the following manner:

---

15 For further study see: a. *God in Three Persons*, Carl Brumback, Pathway Press, Cleveland, Tenn.; b. *Dake's Annotated Reference Bible*, Bible Sales, Inc., Atlanta, Ga.

16 *Webster's New Collegiate Dictionary*, pp. 587, 907, 911.

17 *Ibid.*, p. 909.

18 Henry Clarence Thiessen, *Lectures on Systematic Theology*, Wm. B. Eerdmans Pub. Co., Grand Rapids, 1949, p. 146. Used by permission.

To show that the Holy Spirit is a Person, we note firstly that personal pronouns are used of Him (John 14:17, 16:13, etc.). In the last reference the neuter substantive *pneuma* is referred to by the masculine pronoun *ekeinos,* recognizing the Spirit's personality. The neuter "itself" in Rom. 8:16, 26, has in the A.S.V. been properly changed to "Himself." Secondly, we prove His personality by the name Comforter. The term occurs only in John 14:16, 26; 15:26; 16:7 of the Spirit. It is applied to Christ in John 14:16; 1 John 2:1 (Greek); and since it expresses personality when applied to Christ, it must do so also when applied to the Spirit. Thirdly, we prove it by the personal characteristics ascribed to Him. He has the three essential elements of personality; intellect (1 Cor. 2:11), sensibilities (Rom. 8:27, 15:30), and will (1 Cor. 12:11). Fourthly, we prove the same thing by the personal acts which are said to be performed by Him. He works (1 Cor. 12:11), searches (1 Cor. 2:10), speaks (Acts 13:2; Rev. 2:7), testifies (John 15:26), teaches (John 14:26), reproves (John 16:8-11), regenerates (John 3:5), prays (Rom. 8:26), guides into truth (John 16:13), glorifies Christ (John 16:14), calls man into service (Acts 13:2), and directs him in service (Acts 16:6, 7). Fifthly, His personality is established by the fact of His association with the Father and the Son. This is the case in the baptismal formula (Matt. 28:19), in the Apostolic benediction (2 Cor. 13:14), and in His office as Administrator of the Church (1 Cor. 12:4-6). And finally, we prove His personality by the fact that He is susceptible of personal treatment. He can be tempted (Acts 5:9), lied to (Acts 5:3), grieved (Eph. 4:30; Isa. 63:10, A.S.V.), resisted (Acts 7:51), insulted (Heb. 10:29), and blasphemed (Matt. 12:31, 32). An influence, manifestly, is not susceptible of such treatment. All these things prove that the Holy Spirit is a Person.[19]

---

19 *Ibid.*, p. 144.

"Executive Agent of the Godhead"

"To execute" is to follow through to the end, to complete, to perform, to fulfill in accordance with a design, plan, or the like. It means to effect the will of another.[20] An "agent" refers to a power that acts; a moving force; as, by some other than human agent. It is one who acts for, or in the place of, another, by authority from him.[21]

R. Hollis Gause says,

> The Holy Spirit does not will to make Himself the central figure in the Church or in the consciousness of the individual. He is the Executor of the will of others; namely, the Father and the Son. He is their Spirit; thus He is called the Spirit of God, the Spirit of the Father, the Spirit of the Son, and by other titles indicative of His work. His purpose is to testify of them (John 15:26). The Holy Spirit does not speak of Himself, but what he has heard (John 16:13).[22]

A. J. Gordon refers to the Holy Spirit as the "Divine Agent," as the Executive of the Godhead, as the one Administrator, exercising authority in the ministry and government of the church, in the worship and service of the church, and in the missions of the church. Every believer is sealed and certified as a participant in the death and life of Christ; and the Holy Spirit has been given to be the Executor of the contract.[23]

Lehman Strauss refers to the Holy Spirit as the Divine Agency:

> The Spirit is seen as active in the original creation

---

20 Webster, p. 288.
21 *Ibid.*, p. 17.
22 R. H. Gause, "The Holy Spirit's Relation to the Believer," *Church of God Evangel*, December 10, 1956, p. 7.
23 A. J. Gordon, *The Ministry of the Spirit*, Judson Press, Philadelphia, 1950, pp. 75, 129, 134, 142, 159, 109, 210. Used by permission.

(Job 26:13), in re-creation (Gen. 1:2) and in all creation (Psalm 104:30). In the creation of man, the Spirit is mysteriously and distinctly revealed (Gen. 1:27, 2:7; Job 33:4). The Spirit is involved in the Incarnation of Christ (Luke 1:35; Matt. 1:18, 1:20) and was present at the crucifixion on Calvary (Heb. 9:14). His agency and power were demonstrated in the Resurrection (Rom. 8:11, 1 Peter 3:18), and in Christ's ministry which followed (Acts 1:2).[24]

In his "Dissertations on the Cardinal Truths of Christianity," Joseph Cross speaks of the Holy Ghost as a distinct Agent in the Godhead:

The whole process of our spiritual illumination and renovation is effected by His gracious agency. It is a work which no other agency could accomplish. What was the reason for the expediency of Christ's ascension and the Holy Spirit's outpouring? Christ could have occupied but one locality at a time. The Spirit, confined by no corporeal investiture, can operate everywhere at the same moment. He can operate in the same instant on every human heart. Is this not better? Had He sent twelve legions of angels to minister to every heir of salvation, the agency would have been far less efficient. It is as if Christ had turned Himself into spirit and poured Himself forth upon the world.[25]

Missionary William D. Alton writes,

The Holy Spirit is in His uncreated nature; i.e., He exists on a level alone and beyond matter. He subsists in another mode. His substance has no weight, no dimension, no size, nor existence in space. He is a boundless sea of fire, flowing, moving ever, performing as He moves the eternal purposes of God.[26]

---

24 Lehman Strauss, *The Third Person*, Loizeaux Bros., New York, 1954, pp. 39-42.

25 Joseph Cross, *Headlands of Faith*, Southern Methodist Pub. House, Nashville, Tenn., pp. 198, 205, 208, 209.

26 Lecture on "Glossolalia," William D. Alton, given at the 1967 Servicemen's Retreat in Berchtesgaden, Germany, p. 2.

"The Baptism of the Holy Ghost"

Since the time that Isaiah and Joel predicted an out-pouring upon all flesh, man had longed for the refreshing that would come from God (Isa. 28:11, 12; Joel 2:28, 29). John the Baptist preached and practiced water baptism but alluded to One mightier, who would come later: "He shall baptize you with the Holy Ghost, and with fire" (Matt. 3:11).

This "baptism" is mentioned seven times in the New Testament (Matt. 3:11; Mark 1:8; Luke 3:16; John 1:33; Acts 1:5, 11:16; 1 Cor. 12:13). Christ had spoken of the Spirit baptism on several occasions (John 7:37-39, 14:12-17, 26; 15:26, 16:7-15). The gift of the Holy Spirit on the Day of Pentecost and the miraculous manifestation which followed are clearly the initial historical fulfillment of the baptism of the Holy Spirit (Acts 2:1 ff). In verse 16, Peter declares, "This is that which was spoken by the prophet Joel," and he cites the words of the prophecy from Joel 2:28. When giving the brethren at Jerusalem an account of his visit to the house of Cornelius (Acts 11:16), Peter declares that this event which he had witnessed (Acts 10:44) was a baptism of the Holy Spirit. Evidence that it was not concluded, but that it continued and is a baptism for all who would believe, ask and obey, is seen in numerous scriptural records of which Acts 2:38, 39 and 5:32 are prime examples.

This word "baptize" is taken from the Greek term *baptizo*, meaning to immerse, to submerge, to dip in, etc. . . . The Greeks also used the word to signify the dying of a garment. (Note Acts 1:5.) The Greek text indicates that the upper room in which they were sitting when the Holy Spirit came upon them, was "filled to utmost capacity," by the rushing mighty wind of the Spirit's presence. The disciples were literally "submerged" in the Person of the Holy Ghost.[27] When Pentecostals use the word "baptism" referring to the Holy Ghost, they are referring to the historic moment when the individual was initially filled with the Spirit. They are speaking then of the experiential aspects of the doctrine and actually mean "filled." This is the experience word used in Acts 2:4. The Greek verb from *pimplemi* (filled) indicates that the one hundred and twenty believers experienced the thorough immersion of every faculty, into the Holy Spirit. Its imagery of saturation and satisfaction adequately corresponds to the Pentecostal terminology "baptism of (in) the Holy Ghost" (Matt. 3:11; Acts 1:5, 11:16).[28]

"Charismatic Endowment"

Charisma is a contemporary term that has recently come to be understood in certain strata of our society. It is used as that extra "something" which gives an individual power to attract or gain influence. In recent years the term has especially characterized certain individuals in the political and entertainment world. It refers to a dynamic, a magnetism, a subtle "more than" or "wholly other" characteristic which sets one apart to lead, to be followed, idolized or held in high esteem. This is the secular twentieth century connotation.

Charisma basically means a "gift." Outside the New Testament it is not at all a common word. In classical

---

27 M. G. McLuhan, "The Works of the Holy Ghost in the Life of the Believer," Lecture III, p. 2.

28 Hollis L. Green, "Holy Spirit Baptism," *On Guard*, November 1968, p. 15.

Greek it is rare. It is not common in the papyri, but there is one suggestive occurrence where a man classifies his property as that which he acquired *(apo agorasias)* "by purchase," and that which he acquired *(apo charismatos)* "by gift."[29] The word *charisma*, with a single exception (1 Peter 4:10), occurs in the New Testament only in the Pauline Epistles. In the plural form *(charismata)*, it is employed to denote extraordinary gifts of the Spirit bestowed upon Christians to equip them for service of the church. Various lists of the "charismata" are given in Rom. 12:6-8, 1 Cor. 12:4-11, 28-30 and Eph. 4:7-12.[30] Each of these "gifts" will be dealt with in a later chapter.

The Scriptures differentiate clearly between the "gift" of the Spirit and the "gifts" of the Spirit. In his *Church of God Distinctives*, Dr. Ray H. Hughes states,

> The gifts *(charismata)* of the Spirit are distinct from the gift *(dorea)* of the Holy Ghost. The "charismata" are not to be confused with the Executor or distributor of them.[31]

M. G. McLuhan differentiates between four New Testament designations:

> The Greek word for "gift" is *doran*. It is used of things both temporal and spiritual. It appears in relation to gifts given to support the poor, maintain the temple, of salvation by grace as a gift of God, of the gift of the Holy Ghost as an indwelling person in the believer and of the ministry gifts of the church. In

---

29 William Barclay, *A New Testament Word Book*, Harper & Row, New York, p. 28.

30 *International Standard Bible Encyclopedia*, Vol. V, James Orr, Editor, Howard Severance Co., Chicago, 1929, p. 2843.

31 Ray H. Hughes, *Church of God Distinctives*, Pathway Press, Cleveland, Tenn., 1968, p. 47.

some of these references its derivative *dorea,* meaning "a free gift," is used.

However, in 1 Cor. 12, 13 and 14, neither one of the above Greek words were used. Instead, we find two distinctly different terms, the meaning of which is completely different from that which is generally understood from the word "gift." A gift is something that is given to an individual to be used by him at his own discretion and will. It becomes his forever, and if this is not the case, it is a loan, not a gift. The words used in these chapters in 1 Corinthians do not carry this meaning.

One Greek word used is *pneumatika,* meaning "things of the Spirit" or "enablements of the Spirit." The other word used is "charisma," which comes from the word *charis,* meaning "grace." In other words, these charismatic manifestations are "spiritual endowments" or "graces of the Spirit." They are truly the manifestations of the Holy Ghost "through the believer," as a channel of ministry to the fellowship. They are wrought by the will and initiative of the Holy Spirit "as He wills," not as the believer wills.[32]

The "Charismatic Endowment" does not refer to the gift *(dorea)* of the Holy Ghost which was given on the day of Pentecost (Acts 2). The Charismatic Endowment refers to the gifts *(Charismata)* of the Spirit, as described in 1 Cor. 12. They are endowments which require grace *(charis)* on the part of the donor and on the part of the one exercising the gifts.

"Glossolalia Phenomenon"

Article nine of the Church of God Declaration of Faith states, "We believe. . . In speaking with other tongues as the Spirit gives utterance, and that it is the initial evidence of the baptism of the Holy Ghost."[33]

---

32 McLuhan, *op. cit.,* Lecture IV, p. 1.
33 *1968 Minutes, op. cit.*

The term "glossolalia phenomenon" refers to speaking in tongues. A phenomenon is "an occurrence," or "an actuality." It is from a Greek word meaning "to appear."[34] It is an observable fact or event, an experience as distinguished from a thing-in-itself. It is an exceptional, unusual or abnormal occurrence. Some have considered it an experience or happening which cannot be scientifically explained. Webster calls it "a fact or event of scientific interest susceptible of scientific description or explanation."[35] Dr. R. Leonard Carroll explains the miraculous phenomenon of Acts 2 as being heralded and symbolized by a mysterious sound, an unusual sight and a peculiar touch.[36]

Dr. Charles W. Conn defines "glossolalia" as follows:

> The word is not found in the English translation of the Bible but is based on the Greek word *glossa*, for tongue. The term was used by ancient writers to denote strange or unknown language or speech. The New Testament, written in the Greek, used the expression *glossasis lalein* for the tongues spoken in the Spirit by the earliest Christians. Thus, the present practice of speaking in tongues is known as glossolalia. Those who speak with tongues are known as glossolalists.[37]

Dr. Frank Stagg of the Southern Baptist Theological Seminary explains,

> Speaking in tongues is the popular phrase which scholars term glossolalia. This phenomenon, appearing from time to time in the Christian world, is unmistakably reflected in the New Testament. The noun "glossolalia"

---

34 Harry E. Wedeck, *Classical Word Origins*, Philosophical Library, New York, 1957, p. 58.

35 Webster, p. 632.

36 R. Leonard Carroll, "The Baptism of the Holy Ghost," Evangelism & Home Mission Dept. Brochure, Cleveland, Tenn., 1966.

37 *The Glossolalia Phenomenon*, Wade H. Horton, Editor, Pathway Press, Cleveland, Tenn., 1966, p. 23.

does not appear in the New Testament, but the phrase "to speak with tongues" (*glossasis lalein*) appears, and there are frequent occurrences of the word *glossa*, a component of the term glossolalia. Although *glossa* is commonly translated "tongue" and *lalia* (speaking) for "speaking in tongues," actually the term is employed in at least three different ways: (1) for the physiological organ of taste or speech; (2) for language itself or a manner of speech and (3) for strange or obscure speech.[38]

William D. Alton of Switzerland states,

> Speaking in tongues was instituted by the Lord Jesus Himself. He did not limit the experience to a specific period of time or to a certain group of individuals. "These signs," he said, "shall follow them that believe . . . in my name they shall speak in new tongues" (Mark 16:17).[39]

Dr. Conn warns,

> We must take care not to attach undue significance to glossolalia. The phenomenon has a valid and proper place in the Christian experience, yet it is not an end in itself and should not be sought for its own sake. Tongues would be meaningless in themselves without the deeper Christian life they signify. They would be as meaningless as a herald for a King who does not live or a marker for a place that does not exist.[40]

"The Initial Evidence of the Baptism of the Holy Ghost"

Article nine of the Church of God Declaration of Faith states, "We believe . . . In speaking with other tongues as the Spirit gives utterance and that it is the

---

38 Stagg, Hinson and Oates, *Glossolalia*, Abingdon Press, Nashville, Tenn., 1967, pp. 20, 21, 22.

39 Alton, *op. cit.*

40 Horton, *op. cit.*, p. 25.

initial evidence of the baptism of the Holy Ghost."[41]
Earl P. Paulk, Sr., explains the word "initial" to mean,
placed at the beginning, or first. The word "evidence"
means an outward sign, indication, or that which fur-
nishes proof.[42] Further meaning of the word "initial" is
to mark the commencement.[43]

That glossolalia is the initial, or in the beginning, outward physical evidence that a person has received the
baptism of the Holy Ghost is attested to in numerous
ways. It is alluded to prophetically (Isa. 28:11; Joel
2:28, 29; Mark 16:17; John 15:26, 27, 16:13). It is
validated initially (Acts 2:4). It is established historically (Matt. 18:16; Acts 2:4, 10:44-46, 19:6). It is verified primarily (Acts 2:16, 11:15, 15:8). It is suggest-
ed by context secondarily (Acts 8:18-23, something seen
and heard, Acts 9:17-22, 13:9, 14:18). It is undenied
categorically.* It is reinforced eschatologically (Acts
2:39).

That glossolalia is an initial outward demonstration
of an inward Presence is exegetically sustained.**

Professor R. Hollis Gause translates and explains Acts
2:4:

> And all were filled of the Holy Spirit, and they began
> to speak with other tongues, just as (because) the
> Spirit was giving to them to speak. There was no
> utterance until a specified beginning which is explained
> in the context. The implication here is that there was
> no action on the part of the speakers until this agent

---

41 *1968 Minutes, op. cit.*
42 Earl P. Paulk, Sr., "The Pentecostal Baptism," pp. 7, 8.
43 Webster, p. 432.
* No scriptural reference of denial or suggestion of change.
** To "exegete" is to give a close examination and interpretation of a
portion of scripture.

acted. The cummulative effect is to show that there
was no initiative to speak in other tongues on the part
of the believer; the initiation for this phenomenon was
the action of the Holy Spirit and men could not speak
with other tongues apart from this giving.[44]

The initiative to speak is taken first by the Holy
Spirit; then the believer, as a completely yielded instrument, responds to this stimulus only because the Spirit
takes the initiative.

Dr. Donald B. Gibson explains the use of the word
"for" in Acts 10:46:

> The word "for" in the original is *gar*, which is fre-
> quently used (as it is here) in the illative (inferential)
> sense introducing a reason or evidence.* In such cases
> the evidence attests or enlarges upon a foregoing pre-
> mise. Especially is this clear when the premise con-
> cerns a phenomenon. Representative passages which in-
> volve this type of reasoning are numerous (Matt. 2:2,
> 26:73; John 3:2; Acts 2:15, 8:6, 7, 10:44-46, 28:2).
> This is no new interpretation of the passage, for Pente-
> costal ministers have long held this position. The
> important thing, however, is that the science of lin-
> guistics corroborates a view held by those whose per-
> suasion developed not from reason alone, but from their
> own spiritual experience—the baptism of the Holy
> Ghost.[45]

Initial or in the beginning evidence is not seen as
the "only" evidence. Dr. Ray H. Hughes explains,

> Although the church holds to the position of speaking
> with tongues as the initial evidence of the baptism of
> the Holy Ghost, by no means does it claim that this

---

44 R. H. Gause, "On Acts 2:4," *On Guard*, May 1969, p. 12.
* See Dana and Mantey, *A Manual Grammar of the Greek New Testament*, pp. 243, 274.
45 Donald B. Gibson, "A Pentecostal Strong Point," *Church of God
Evangel*, May 15, 1961, p. 7.

is the only evidence that one has been baptized with
the Holy Ghost. The Spirit does not come merely to
speak, but the speaking is His announcement that He
has come to the believer and will accompany him in
performing the task of implementing the Great Commission. Speaking in tongues is not the zenith of the
believer's experience, but a beginning of more effective
service and a more powerful witnessing for Jesus
Christ.[46]

James L. Slay reassures,

We would like for all mankind to know that we hold
speaking in other tongues to be the initial evidence, but
not the only evidence of the baptism of the Holy Ghost.
If there have been those who felt that tongues was
thought by the Church of God to be the only evidence,
they were not quite right. There may have been some
who innocently overemphasized the "tongues" experience, but never have we felt that the initial evidence
was the only evidence.[47]

Editor Lewis J. Willis emphasizes,

Pentecostals believe that the speaking with tongues is
the initial, empirical evidence of the baptism in the Holy
Ghost. They do not believe that speaking in tongues is
the only evidence, nor do they hold that in and of
itself speaking in tongues constitutes the "fullness of
the Spirit." They simply believe that glossolalia is the
first overt and audible evidence that one has been
baptized in the Holy Spirit.
Primarily, Pentecostals do not magnify glossolalia, but
rather the encompassing benefits of the baptism with the
Holy Ghost. Those who are really baptized of the
Spirit will soon be engaged in the collaborating evidence—that of witnessing for Christ. The experience

46 Hughes, *op. cit.*, p. 37.
47 Slay, *op. cit.*, p. 88.

of the baptism of the Holy Ghost is not an end in itself but only a means to an end—pointing men to Christ.[48]

M. G. McLuhan asks,

What other one of the nine "spirituals" or "gifts" would be suitable as an initial evidence? We must conclude that speaking with other tongues as the Holy Spirit gives the utterance, is the only scriptural "initial evidence" of the baptism in the Holy Ghost. There are many subsequent evidences, including the eight spirituals named, but they manifest themselves as they are needed, and not as initial proofs of the Pentecostal experience.[49]

Donald Gee writes,

All the distinctive manifestations of the Day of Pentecost were not repeated and need not be expected. They are unnecessary. The Comforter has come and abides, but be it noted that enough is repeated to make subsequent Pentecosts recognizable as such. The Scriptures do not refer anymore to a rushing mighty wind, or cloven tongues like as of fire but they do refer to speaking with other tongues as the Spirit gives utterance.[50]

William G. McDonald reiterates,

It is possible that the sound of the wind that attracted the first crowd on the day of Pentecost had subsided and the fire had vanished before the mockers (Acts 2:13) arrived, but the glossolalia remained as a "sign" to them (Mark 16:17; 1 Cor. 14:22). Significantly, glossolalia is repeated in other instances of the Spirit's outpouring throughout the book of Acts, whenever the writer tells in detail what happens when people initially receive the Holy Spirit. Glossolalia may well have

[48] Lewis J. Willis, "What Your Pentecostal Neighbor Believes," *Church of God Evangel*, May 27, 1968, p. 13.

[49] McLuhan, *op. cit.*, pp. 2, 4.

[50] Donald Gee, "Pentecost, a Word With Many Meanings," *Pentecostal Evangel*, March 21, 1965, p. 6.

been the norm in all the churches that Paul founded, in that it was not such an uncommon thing that it had to be specified every time it occurred.[51]

OUTLINE OF PENTECOSTAL FACTS

Record	Time	Place	Who	Minister	How	What Happened?	Evidence
Acts 2:4	A.D. 33	Jerusalem	120 disciples (Hebrews)	Peter	Tarried, praising and blessing God. Lk. 24:53	Filled with the Holy Ghost	Began to speak in other tongues
8:17	34	Samaria	Samaritans (Mixed breeds)	Peter and John	Laying on of hands	Received the Holy Ghost	Note No. 1
9:18	35	Damascus	One Jew Saul	Ananias	Laying on of hands	Note No. 2	Note No. 2
10:44	41	Caesarea	Italians (Gentiles)	Peter	Hearing of faith	Holy Ghost fell on all that heard	They heard them speak in tongues
19:6	54	Ephesus	12 Jews	Paul	Laying on of hands	Holy Ghost came upon them	They spake with tongues

Note No. 1. Simon witnessed some evidence of spiritual power for which he offered money.
Note No. 2. Paul said, "I speak with tongues more than ye all." I Cor. 14:18

"Power"

Article eight of the Church of God teachings in its *Minutes* states that we believe in the "baptism of the Holy Ghost subsequent to cleansing; the enduement of power for service (Matt. 3:11; Luke 24:49, 53; Acts 1:4-8)."

Dr. Ray H. Hughes says,

The word for power in this Scripture (Acts 1:8) is *dunamis*. It is derived from a word which signifies ability—the power to accomplish anything. Hence it is frequently translated, "is able," "can do" or "possibility to do a thing."[52]

Dunamis is further defined as power in action. That power of God which manifests itself in all modes of His work—redeeming, revealing, carrying out His plan; that ability to effect all divine purposes.[53] It refers to "potency," "possibility" or power that can be applied over the

51 William G. McDonald, "Glossolalia in Acts Analyzed," *On Guard*, October 1969, pp. 8, 10.
52 Ray H. Hughes, *What Is Pentecost?*, Pathway Press, Cleveland, Tenn., 1963, p. 42.
53 Bullinger, *A Critical Lexicon and Concordance*, Bagster & Sons Limited, London, 1957, p. 593.

whole range of life, such as physical, intellectual, moral and spiritual.[54] This power is seen as a living Presence in the believer (Rom. 15:13; 2 Cor. 13:3ff). It is seen as the life energy of the Eternal One flowing into and out from believers. God grants them power of His Spirit to accomplish with Him His saving purpose for the world. Dr. Paul S. Rees described (1) the Holy Spirit as "the source," (2) the power as "the force," and (3) unto the uttermost as "the course."[55]

Dr. R. Leonard Carroll observes,

> The power of the Holy Ghost has never been measured, weighed or surmised. One breath of God can erase and create simultaneously. Being invisible, the Holy Ghost fits into the category of the most powerful forces.[56]

Wade H. Horton says,

> There is no question but that the force of this Pentecostal experience has been felt from the day of Pentecost until now. Jesus instructed His followers to tarry in Jerusalem, "until ye be endued with power from on high" (Luke 24:49). Again in Acts 1:8, He states, "But ye shall receive power after that the Holy Ghost is come upon you. . . ." They were to be endued with a mighty supernatural force—a force outside themselves; a force direct from the throne of God; a power of dynamite proportion, adequate to meet all opposition and obstacles.[57]

The Holy Ghost Himself is the power, when you have

54 Gerhard Kittel, Editor, *Theological Dictionary of the New Testament,* Vol. II, Wm. B. Eerdmans Pub. Co., Grand Rapids, 1964, p. 285. Used by permission.

55 Paul S. Rees, "The Holy Spirit and the Church's Mission," *World Vision,* April 1961, p. 6.

56 R. Leonard Carroll, "The Occasion—Pentecost," *Church of God Evangel,* May 9, 1966, p. 13.

57 Wade H. Horton, "The Promise of Pentecost," *Church of God Evangel,* May 18, 1964, p. 8.

Him you have all the power you need to do anything God wants you to do.

"Paraclete"

The word *Paraclete* is used as a title for both the Second and Third Persons of the Holy Trinity. It means "called to one's aid," implying capability or adaptation for giving aid.[58] *Paraclete* is simply a Greek word transferred into English. It is taken from the verb *kaleo,* meaning "to call" and the prepositional prefix *para* meaning "beside, or along side of."[59] *Para* carries with it the idea of close personal association.[60] The word occurs five times in the New Testament, all in the writings of John. Four instances are in the Gospel (John 14:16, 26; 15:26; 16:7) and one in the Epistle (1 John 2:1). Most translations of this word in the Gospel is "Comforter" and in the Epistle it is "Advocate."

An analysis of the varied translations of the same word describes "Comforter" as too narrow, as the work of the paraclete was more than to comfort in sorrow. "Intercessor" comes nearer the root idea and "Advocate" is closely related and suggestive of the work of the Spirit. Perhaps there is no English word broad enough to cover all the significance of *Paraclete* except the word "Helper." Of course the objection here is that it is too indefinite. The conclusion is that the word *Paraclete* itself would be the best designation of the Spirit in John's Gospel. It would, thus, become a proper name for the Spirit and the various meanings would come from the context of the Gospel.[61]

---

58 Bullinger, *op. cit.,* p. 168.

59 Vine, *op. cit.,* pp. 207, 208.

60 Kenneth S. Wuest, *The Practical Use of the Greek N. T.,* Moody Press, Chicago, 1946, p. 70.

61 I.S.B.E., Vol. IV, p. 2245.

Christ uses the word to refer to "another Comforter" as One who is to take His place. The word "another" is from the Greek *allos,* meaning another of the same sort, not *heteras,* another of a different sort.[62] Dr. G. H. C. Macgregor finely puts it, "The Spirit is Christ's alter ego."[63] It means One who takes the place of, a second "I" or a second "self," a self same "other one."

William Barclay best analyzes this word of the Holy Spirit by explaining the multiple meanings of *Paraclete.*

> The function of the Holy Spirit is to fill a man with that which would make him able triumphantly to cope with life. If he needs someone to plead his cause, the Paraclete will be an Advocate. If he needs consoling, the Spirit will help his infirmities and make intercession for him. If he needs advice, He will be a Counselor. Always the purpose of "calling someone in" was that they might do something, render some service. The call was like one to public duty. Like calling and assigning a coach to maintain and train a team at his own expense.
>
> A man, in a situation with which he cannot cope, calls in a "helper." Now, he is more than able to cope with the dilemma. Job's "miserable comforters" (Job 16:2) worked in contrast to the Holy Spirit's comfort. The work of the Spirit is the opposite to the miserable comforters of Job. His, is a rallying call to the troops from the General. He incites to action, puts courage into the fainthearted, nerve into the feeble arm, and exhorts the soldier to accept the risks of battle. He keeps a man on his two feet and enables him to pass the breaking point and not to break.[64]

R. Hollis Gause defines the *Paraclete* as a term for both the Person of Jesus Christ and the Person of the

---

62 Vine, *op. cit.,* p. 208.
63 William Barclay, *More New Testament Words,* Harper & Row, New York, 1958, p. 133.
64 *Ibid.,* pp. 130-135.

Holy Spirit. "The Holy Ghost, the invisible divine Helper, is to the Church the world over what Christ was to the small body of disciples."[65]

Thus, *Paraclete* becomes "the word of the Holy Spirit" and as an eclectic, chooses from the English concepts of Comforter, Advocate, Intercessor, Teacher, Guide, Helper, et cetera, as needed to assist the one He indwells. This is illustrated by the ancient armor-bearer. An armor-bearer was the warrior's constant companion in battle. He was ready with whatever defensive or offensive weapon that was needed.

I think most significantly the *Paraclete* means "presence." The Holy Spirit actually became the personal substitute for Christ's own self. How beautifully it was acknowledged at the first council at Jerusalem (Acts 15:28): "It seemed good to the Holy Ghost, and to us" —His meeting with and counseling with them, and all coming to a common conclusion! How real the sense of His presence when Peter can say to Ananias, "Why hath Satan filled thine heart to lie to the Holy Ghost," as though He stood there, behind Peter as the real presiding Officer! How reassuring it is to experience the abiding presence of the *Parakletos*—the one called along beside. Did not Jesus say, "I will not leave you orphans *(orphanos)* . . . I will come . . . to you." (John 14:18, Amplified New Testament.)

"Pentecost"

The word "pentecost" is taken from the Greek word *pentekostos*. *Pente,* an adjective denoting five of fiftieth, is used as a noun with "day" understood, i.e. the fiftieth

---

65 R. H. Gause, "The Ministry of the Holy Spirit in the Life of the Individual," *Church of God Evangel*, May 8, 1967, pp. 4, 5.

day.[66] In the Old Testament, as the name indicates, Pentecost was observed on the fiftieth day from the Paschal Feast.[67] It was one of the three great Jewish festivals celebrated by Israel. It followed the Passover and preceded the Feast of Tabernacles. This Ceremonial Pentecost had numerous identifying characteristics. First, it was celebrated the fiftieth day from the first Sunday after the Passover (Lev. 23:15). Second, it was observed the fiftieth day after the presentation of the first harvested sheaf of the barley harvest (Lev. 23:10, 15; Deut. 16:9). Third, it was known as "the feast of weeks" (Ex. 34:22, Deut. 16:10), because it was held after a completion of seven weeks each marked by seven days which denotes completeness. Fourth, it was the day of the firstfruits (Ex. 23:16, Num. 28:26) because this was the day when the firstfruits of the wheat harvest (Ex. 34:22) were presented to God. Fifth, it was a day of cheer and joy, of liberal giving to the Levite and the poor, of remembering their former bondage and a day of reconsecration to the Lord. Sixth, it was a foreshadow of something greater that was to follow.

The old Jewish Ceremonial Festival acquired renewed significance in the New Testament. It was on the Day of Pentecost that the Holy Spirit was first poured out upon the Early Church (Acts 2:1-3). This initial baptism of Pentecost was a fulfilling of prophecy and the promise and prayer of Christ (Isa. 28:11; Joel 2:28, 29; Luke 24:49; John 14:16, 26; Acts 1:4, 5); hence the expression "Pentecostal experience." In the Christian Church, Pentecost is the anniversary of the coming of the Holy Spirit. It is a Christian Festival commemorating

---

66 Vine, *op. cit.*, p. 172.
67 I.S.B.E., Vol. IV, p. 2318.

the descent of the Holy Spirit. It is significant that this particular Day of Pentecost was fifty days after Christ's crucifixion, seven weeks after His resurrection and ten days after His ascension into heaven (Acts 1:2, 3).

For all generations of Christians, Pentecost will stand for the great initial outpouring of the Holy Spirit. It is also the first account of speaking in tongues. It is admitted by all that the phenomenon of speaking in tongues did not occur in the Old Testament or Gospel periods and that it first happened on the day of Pentecost (Acts 2). When the Holy Spirit filled the disciples on the day of Pentecost, they began to speak with other tongues as the Spirit gave them utterance (Acts 2:4).[68] This is not all they began. Pentecost was not an end, but a beginning. Every subsequent personal "Pentecost" became not an end, but a beginning. It was the beginning of a great harvest and ingathering of souls to Christ. All local and personal "Pentecosts" should find their "norm" in the Scriptural Pentecosts "as at the beginning" (Acts 11:15, 15:8).

What is a Pentecostal? It is someone who has experienced the same blessings that the New Testament Christians received, including the baptism of the Holy Ghost as received on the Day of Pentecost according to Acts 2. The Pentecostal way is the New Testament way.

What is the Pentecostal Movement or Pentecostalism? According to John Thomas Nichol,

> Pentecostalism is a movement that boldly maintains that a Holy Spirit baptism that is accompanied by the evi-

---

68 Robert G. Gromacki, *The Modern Tongues Movement*, Presbyterian & Reform, Philadelphia, 1967, p. 59.

dential sign of "speaking in tongues" is a normative religious experience available to all Christians.[69]

Speaking of the rapid growth of Pentecostalism in the Twentieth Century, Robert G. Gromacki quotes the following sources:

> *Time* called it the fastest growing church in the hemisphere. *Life* regarded it as "the third force," equal in significance to Roman Catholicism and historic Protestantism. Henry P. Van Dusen, past president of Union Theological Seminary (New York), felt that the Pentecostal movement with its emphasis upon the Holy Spirit was a revolution comparable in importance with the establishment of the original Apostolic Church and with the Protestant Reformation.[70]

While Pentecostalism now receives wide acclaim and the term has acquired many new uses, it should be understood that twentieth century neo-pentecostalism is not necessarily the same as "Pentecost" or synonymous with the New Testament way.

Who started or founded the contemporary Pentecostal Movement? Historian, Dr. Charles W. Conn explains,

> No man or group of men can be pointed to as founder of the Pentecostal movement—it just didn't happen that way. No one locality can be pointed out as the birthplace of the movement—it was born spontaneously over most of the world during the decade 1896-1906. In the manner of the Protestant Reformation and the Methodist Revival, the Pentecostal movement came into existence without being planned.[71]

The oldest Pentecostal church in America is the Church of God. Its existence dates from 1886 when it began.

---

69 John Thomas Nichol, *Pentecostalism*, Harper & Row, New York, 1966, p. 11.

70 Gromacki, *op. cit.*, p. 2.

71 Charles W. Conn, *Pillars of Pentecost*, Pathway Press, Cleveland, Tenn., 1956, p. 22.

A recurrence of Pentecost fell unexpectedly on humble, sincere seekers in a revival led by a layman in the Camp Creek area of North Carolina in 1896, ten years prior to the outpouring of the Holy Ghost in California in 1906, which is popularly regarded as the beginning of the modern Pentecostal movement.[72]

The most important Pentecost is a personal one. A Pentecost that you and I must have here and now, and it is ours for the asking.

72 Conn, *Like A Mighty Army,* Church of God Publishing House, Cleveland, Tenn., 1955, pp. 24, 25.

2

The Holy Spirit in Experience

"And when he is come"

To experience is to actually live through an event.
It will not be the purpose of this chapter to enumerate
or to classify spiritual experiences. The ministries and
works of the Holy Spirit are multiple. It is the purpose
of this chapter to point out basic experiences in which
the Holy Spirit is involved in bringing about man's salvation, his establishment in the faith and his empower-
ment for service in the kingdom. Lewis J. Willis states,
"The Holy Spirit is essential in the whole process by
which man is brought to Christ, established in the
Christian faith and prepared as a faithful witness of
Christ whom He has made Lord of his life."[1]

M. G. McLuhan explains,

> Though our statement of faith and our teachings may
> clearly show the work of the Holy Ghost in spiritual
> birth, sanctification and the Pentecostal baptism, we

---

1 Willis, *op. cit.*, p. 5.

have sometimes left the impression that the Holy
Spirit has no contact with the believer until he speaks
with other tongues as the Spirit gives the utterance.
This of course is not our true position.[2]

Since the Holy Spirit is seen as the Agent in all true
Christian experience (Romans 14:17), we will deal
with the Holy Spirit in revelation, conviction, conversion,
sanctification, the Holy Spirit baptism and the enduement of power for service.

"In Revelation"

"Revelation" means God's disclosure or manifestation
of Himself and His will to man. To reveal is to unveil,
it implies the lifting up of a curtain so all can see alike
what is uncovered. The Spirit is the Agent of revelation
(Eph. 1:17). Revelations are by the Spirit and not
flesh and blood (Matt. 16:17). The proper subject of
revelation is God, His being and His works. God cannot
be observed, He must be revealed.[3]

The Holy Spirit was *first* involved in revelation
through the creation. Numerous scriptural passages point
to God's revelation in His creation and to the Holy Spirit's action in this experience (Gen. 1:2; Job 26:13; Psa.
19:1-4, 104:30; Rom. 1:18-20). Our self-centeredness
often tempts us to restrict the work of the Spirit to ourselves. He works, however, through all vital media to
communicate God to us and His communiques do not
contradict.

The *finest* revelation of God is Jesus Christ, the In-
carnate One. He was God in the flesh (John 1:14;
Rom. 8:3; Phil. 2:6-8). When man needed to see again

---

2 McLuhan, *op. cit.*, Lecture 1, p. 2.
3 Richardson, *op. cit.*, pp. 196, 198.

what God was like and God desired to see again what He originally intended man to be—He sent Jesus! Revelation is to be found in the whole fact of Christ.[4]

The scriptures give testimony to the Spirit's presence in Christ's birth (Matt. 1:18, 20; Luke 1:35, 41; 2:25, 26), baptism (Matt. 3:16; John 1:32, 33), temptation (Matt. 4:1; Mark 1:12; Luke 4:1), public ministry (Luke 4:18-21), death and resurrection (Heb. 9:14; Rom. 1:4, 8:11).

The Bible is the *final* revelation of God. It is the final authority by which all revelations are verified. It was fulfilled, endorsed, quoted and proclaimed by Jesus (John 5:39). The Bible is God's self-revelation or self-disclosure. Dr. Donald Aultman illustrates,

> No matter how well one may be acquainted with a friend, there are certain things he can never know about unless he chooses to disclose these intimate facts about himself. By the same principle God revealed to man intimate knowledge of Himself through self-revelation of inspired Scripture.[5]

The Holy Spirit is the Agent in this revelation (2 Peter 1:21). The prophets uttered things far beyond their knowledge and searched diligently for the meaning (1 Peter 1:10-12). Peter emphasizes his confidence in the Scriptures. "We have a more sure word of prophecy; whereunto ye do well that ye take heed, as unto a light that shineth in a dark place" (2 Peter 1:19).

Living Letters paraphrases,

> The whole Bible was given to us by inspiration from God and is useful to teach us what is true and to

---

4 *Ibid.*, p. 197.

5 Donald S. Aultman, *The Ministry of Christian Teaching*, Pathway Press, Cleveland, Tennessee, 1966, p. 35.

make us realize what is wrong in our lives; it straightens us out and helps us to do what is right. It is God's way of making us well-prepared at every point, fully equipped to do good to everyone (2 Tim. 3:16, 17).[6]

In his search for an easy way out, man has often fallen prey to a hunch, a so-called voice or special revelation. When God's Spirit gave us the Bible, He gave us the only infallible Guidebook. It is replete with solutions for all situations and is God's "manual for living." One of its greatest assets is its permanency. Visions, dreams and experiences come and go. How vague and distorted they become even after a few days. The "inscripturation" of the revelation gives man a permanent record of God's manifestation of Himself, something that has not become vague or abstract and will not become distorted (Matt. 24:35; Psa. 119:89). In a certain sense, we are more fortunate than the people who saw and heard. We have His voice with us permanently.

Necessary for understanding the Guidebook is a teacher who knows and can teach the Book. Sometimes we can't read it straight or make it work—it's like trying to tell time on a ticking clock at night, we need someone to turn on the light. The Holy Spirit turns on the light. He illuminates the dark passages (1 Cor. 2:14). He is the teacher of His Book (John 14:26). He is the Guide who knows the way (John 14:17, 15:26, 16:13). Sometimes we know not what to say. It is the Spirit that teaches us (Luke 12:11, 12). Sometimes we know not how to pray. It is the Spirit that helps us (Rom. 8:26, 27). Dr. Aultman writes, "Secular education views its task as being dialogical (two persons in communica-

---

6 Kenneth Taylor, *Living Letters*, Tyndale House Publishers, 1962, pp. 229, 230.

tion), but the Christian educator knows that his work is not a dialogue but a trialogue or perhaps even a multi-logue."[7]

The Holy Spirit is present in the encounter of the Word with the heart and mind of man. His presence accompanies the Word which He inspired. He enlightens it as lightning the precipice to the night traveler, as the sun the landscape which was there before but hidden.

The revelation is final. There is to be no more adding to or taking from (Rev. 22:18, 19). Any continuing revelation of God by the Spirit will conform in all essentials to that which the prophets and apostles bore testimony.[8] But, you ask, does God not speak to men today? Yes, primarily through His Word. There are other ways in which He speaks, but in every case the message conforms to the Bible. How about visions and dreams? Yes, the Bible teaches these (Acts 2:17). But be assured that these are not to supercede, go beyond, replace or contradict "Thus saith the Lord" in His Holy Word. We need to distinguish between God's revelation and our fancies. This is why God gave us the Word as "a standard" by which to try the spirits (1 John 4:1). We are still finite and need authority—that authority is the Bible—the Word of God.

"In Conviction"

It is the work of the Holy Spirit to reprove the world of sin, and of righteousness, and of judgment (John 16:8). The word "reprove" is from *elegcho* meaning to convict, convince, expose to shame or to rebuke.

---

7 Aultman, *op. cit.,* p. 75.
8 Richardson, *op. cit.,* p. 199.

> The New Testament usage is simple and straightforward. It means to show someone his sin and to summon him to repentance. It is the experience of the sinner when faced by the prophet who demands repentance (Luke 3:19; 1 Cor. 14:24). The word does not mean only "to blame" or "to reprove" but "to set right" namely "to point away from sin to repentance." It implies educative discipline.[9]

Conviction as an experience will therefore be presented as it relates to the sinner, the Spirit and the saint.

Mathis describes *the condition of the sinner* as (1) sinful, (2) enslaved, (3) blind, and (4) dead.[10] In the Cotton Patch Version of Paul's Epistles, Clarence Jordan translates, "If our good news is unclear, it is unclear only to those whose lives are falling apart at the seams. They have let the god of things blind their faithless minds so that the illumination of the glorious good news of Christ, who is the very image of God, could not penetrate them (2 Cor. 4:3, 4)"[11]

If, on a cloudless day, you showed someone the sun and asked, "What do you see?" And he replied, "Nothing at all." You would say to yourself, "He's blind" (2 Cor. 4:3, 4). If blinded man is ever to see, he must have an operation performed on his spiritual eyes. This is what the Holy Ghost does. Vep Ellis exclaimed,

> He opened up my blinded eyes and then I had a
>   great surprise,
> I'm in a new world since the Lord saved me.

Is it any wonder we sing,

---

9 Kittle, *op. cit.*, pp. 473, 474.

10 C. Wade Freeman, *The Holy Spirit's Ministry,* Zondervan Publishers, Grand Rapids, 1954, pp. 18, 19.

11 Clarence Jordan, *The Cotton Patch Version of Paul's Epistles,* Association Press, New York, 1968, p. 79.

> I once was lost, but now I'm found,
> Was blind but now I see.

The Spirit illuminates and intensifies the truth. God cannot make the truth any more true. If change is wrought, it is not in the truth, but in the soul of man.

Never to be forgotten was my first stroll on that open air portico of the General Walker Hotel in Berchtesgaden, Germany. Earlier that morning when Roosevelt Miller and I had looked out of the window, all we could see was a haze. Now the sun was shining, the haze had lifted and I saw the "Alps," a scene which I shall never forget. "The New Testament uses this word *convict* to describe the work of the Holy Spirit by which the satanic blindness is lifted from men's eyes, and they see themselves as they are in God's sight."[12]

> Open mine eyes that I may see glimpses of truth Thou
>   hast for me;
> Place in my hand the wonderful key that shall unclasp
>   and set me free.
> Silently now I wait for Thee, ready, O God, Thy
>   will to be;
> Open mine eyes, illumine me, Spirit Divine!

It is the condition of the sinner that necessitates *the conviction of the Spirit.* One cannot be saved until he feels conviction for his sins (Luke 18:13). "The Spirit acts as Christ's 'prosecuting attorney,' working to secure a divine conviction against the rejecters of Christ. To convict means to bring home truths otherwise doubted or discarded."[13] "The Holy Spirit convicts by proof, presenting such evidence sufficient to convict if it does not

---

12 Rees, *Bakers Book of Theology, op. cit.,* p. 140.
13 Pearlman, *op. cit.,* p. 303.

convince, and to condemn if it does not convert. . . ."[14]
"This is not wrought by referring us to Josephus or
Tacitus. The content of the Scripture is brought to the
soul. The conflict between the Word and the soul is
felt. The conviction wrought, causes us to see not that
the Scripture must make room for us, but we for the
Scripture."[15]

He convicts of the meaning of sin. Jesus said, "Because
they believe not on me," making unbelief the "Mother
sin" (John 16:9). Where it continues all other sins are
retained, and when it departs, all other sins are removed.

> What good does it do to plead against this sin or the
> other sin, when the soul is not right with God? No
> sooner do we patch up the life here than it breaks
> out in a new place yonder. Small and meager is the
> result when we minister to the pimples on the skin
> while the disease is in the bloodstream that courses
> through the heart. There is but one sin, Mother to all
> the rest and that sin is lack of faith in the blessed
> Lord Jesus.[16]

"It is not necessarily the sin question, so much as it is
the Son question. Christ perfectly satisfied God about
sin, the question now between God and man is: 'Are
you perfectly satisfied with Christ?' "[17] "Far removed
from a character building program, or merely an en-
couragement to live more righteously, the Holy Spirit
reveals that it is necessary to believe in Christ to be
saved."[18]

---

14 James Buchanan, *The Office and Work of the Holy Spirit*, The
Banner of Truth and Trust, London, 1966, p. 27.

15 Kuyper, *op. cit.*, p. 178.

16 W. A. Criswell, *The Holy Spirit in Today's World*, Zondervan Publishers, Grand Rapids, 1966, pp. 88, 89.

17 Gordon, *op. cit.*, p. 191.

18 John F. Walvoord, *The Holy Spirit*, Dunham Publishing Company,
Grand Rapids, 1958, p. 113.

A new understanding of sin will bring a new conviction about righteousness. The conviction that our righteousness is as "filthy rages," and that God provides for our lack by imputing (reckoning, accounting) Christ's righteousness to us (1 Cor. 1:30), making it possible for God to deal with us as those who *are* righteous.

The Spirit also brings man into judgment. It takes place in the heart. Before the bar of justice he stands condemned and on the cinder path that terminates at hell's gate. Calvary looms before the consciousness and he sees Christ hanging on a tree, judged in his stead, executed in his place. It is then the light of salvation shines through and he can see Christ, "the way, the truth, and the life." Not only has Satan been judged and foiled, but his plan for man's life has been defeated. Christ has made the difference.

How, then, is the condition of the sinner and the conviction of the Spirit *the concern of the Saint?*

First, it is only the Spirit that convicts. We cannot convict people of their sins. It is the Holy Spirit that does the work of convicting men. Dr. James A. Cross, preaching in the World Pentecostal Conference at Jerusalem said, "This work of convicting souls is not our own work, but the blessed office work of the Holy Ghost. Your powerful sermons, pulpit mannerisms, magnetisms and orations are of little avail if Pentecost is not perpetuated (Acts 2:37). A. B. Simpson said, 'We can rebuke the world but He alone can convict it.' "[19]

This simply means that the Sword of the Spirit is best wielded by the Spirit (Heb. 4:12). Kuyper explains,

---

19 James A. Cross, "Pentecost Perpetuated," *Church of God Evangel,* July 10, 1961, p. 6.

> The Holy Spirit plies this conviction. He puts the twoedged sword directly upon the heart. The sinner is inclined to shrink from that sword, to let it glance harmlessly from the soul. But then the Holy Spirit continues to press that sword of conviction, driving it so forcibly into the soul that at last, it cuts through and takes effect.[20]

"For as God alone can properly bear witness to His own records, so these words will not obtain full credit in the hearts of men until they are sealed by the inward testimony of the Spirit."[21]

Second, the Saints are the primary channels through which the Spirit convicts. "While it is the Holy Spirit who convicts men . . . He does it though us, i.e., through those who already believe on Jesus Christ. The Holy Spirit comes to the believer, and through the believer convinces the unsaved."[22]

> Does not our Lord say, ". . . whom the world cannot receive." "If I depart, I will send him unto you. And when he is come [to you], he will reprove the world." Connecting this promise with the Great Commission (Mark 16:15), we may conclude that when the Lord sends His messengers into the world, the Spirit of truth goes with them, witnessing to the message which they bear, convincing of the sin which they reprove, and revealing the righteousness which they proclaim.[23]

"The saint is the middle man in the economy of grace, he is God's contact man, the connecting link between the Spirit and the sinner (Rom. 10:13, 14; Acts 10; 11:12-15)."[24]

---

20 Kuyper, *op. cit.*, p. 347.
21 Alan Richardson, *Christian Apologetics*, Harper & Row, New York, 1947, p. 212.
22 R. A. Torrey, *The Holy Spirit*, Fleming H. Revell Co., New York, 1927, pp. 59, 60.
23 Gordon, *op. cit.*, pp. 187, 188.
24 Freeman, *op. cit.*, pp. 23-25.

Third, before we can be channels of conviction to others we must be convicted ourselves. The messenger must feel his message. George Fox said, "I preach what I do feel." We have no right to preach anything we do not feel. Jesus wept over Jerusalem. How do you feel about your community? Louis Evans tells of Luther, Macaulay and Booth:

> As Luther stood looking at a painting of the crucifixion of Christ, he cried out in deepest emotion, "My God! My God! For me, for me!" Macaulay was so upset on seeing the slaves of Sierra Leone that he could not sleep for days. William Booth was so emotionally stirred by the sight of the drunks in the London gutters that he could neither eat nor sleep for a week. These men felt—and then they shook the world![25]

Finally, the Spirit will not always strive with man (Gen. 6:3). While He is the inescapable Spirit as far as finding us (Psa. 139:1, 2), He will not forever strive with us. This makes the responsibility of the believer even more acute. Christian Workers, the time for our task is limited. We must depend upon the Spirit in all that we do (Zech. 4:6).

"In Conversion"

Church of God Teachings, one through four, refer to (1) Repentance, (2) Justification, (3) Regeneration and (4) the New birth.[26] Article four of the Statement of Truth adopted in 1948 by the Pentecostal Fellowship of North America states, "We believe that for the salvation of the lost and sinful men regeneration by the Holy Spirit is absolutely essential." This, along with other

---

25 Louis H. Evans, *Life's Hidden Power*, Fleming H. Revell Co., 1958, pp. 35-38.
26 *1968 Minutes, op. cit.*, p. 6.

articles, was taken from the Statement of Faith as drawn up in 1943 by the National Association of Evangelicals.[27] It is interesting to note that seven of the eight PFNA statements are from the NAE, which reiterates five of the famous "Five Articles of Fundamentalism." The articles of PFNA and NAE are cited in that the Church of God is a member of these cooperative groups.

What is conversion? It is referred to generally as being born again, saved or regenerated. Conviction is not conversion. When a person is convicted of his sin by the Holy Spirit, he may do one of two things: he may harden his heart and resist the overtures of the Spirit, or he may yield, open his heart and invite Christ in as Lord of his life. While conviction is not conversion, few people reach this point without going all the way with Christ (Acts 24:25; Matt. 27:3).

Meyer Pearlman explains this divine act which imparts the newer and higher life as:

> (1) A Birth (1 John 5:1; John 3:7, 8), (2) A Cleansing (Titus 3:5), (3) A Quickening (Col. 3:10; Rom. 12:2; Eph. 4:23), (4) A Creation (2 Cor. 5:17; Eph. 4:24) and (5) A Resurrection (Rom. 6:4, 5; Eph. 2:5, 6). Which comes first, regeneration or conversion? The operations are deep and mysterious and should not be analyzed with mathematical precision. Dr. Strong tells of a candidate for ordination who was asked which comes first and he replied, "They are like the cannon ball and the hole—they both go through together."[28]

Regeneration is *indispensable*. It is not optional (Matt. 18:3; John 3:3). There is an inflexibility to the imperative of the new birth. Ruth Paxton says, "Jesus

---

27 Nichol, *op. cit.*, pp. 4, 5.
28 Pearlman, *op. cit.*, pp. 242, 243, 227.

shows the utter impossibility of making the flesh spiritual
(1 John 3:6). It may be moral flesh, cultured flesh,
traveled flesh and even religious flesh, but it is still
flesh."[29] The answer is its crucifixion, mortification and
resurrection through the new birth (Rom. 8:13; Col.
3:5). There are absolutely no exceptions to this funda-
mental requirement. As Walter Pettitt puts it, "It is the
'one must' of the Bible. The new birth is the only way
to heaven."[30]

Regeneration is *instantaneous* (John 3:6; 5:24). This
simply says either you are saved or you are not. Conviction might be a process, but conversion is a point
where you turn and walk no more in the direction you
were walking. Dr. Donald N. Bowdle says, "It is instantaneous in that regeneration, a restoration to life which
issues in restatement to divine favor, occupies but one
blessed moment."[31] Born-again believers can truthfully
sing,

> I can tell you the time, I can take you to the place,
> Where the Lord saved me by His wonderful grace.

Regeneration is also *inclusive* (2 Cor. 5:17). True
conversion will involve the total being. It will be a complete radical change, the great reversal, a metamorphosis
that is a total transformation. You will have a change
of motives, attitudes, priorities and conduct; a change of
masters, commitments and associations. The things you
once hated you now love and the things you once loved
you now hate. The change will be revolutionary. More

29 Ruth Paxton, *Life on the Highest Plane*, Vol. II, Moody Press, Moody
Bible Institute of Chicago, 1928, p. 44. Used by permission.
30 Walter Pettitt, "The New Birth," Evangelism and Home Missions
Dept., Cleveland, Tenn.
31 Donald N. Bowdle, "The Holy Spirit in Regeneration," *Church of
God Evangel*, September 27, 1965, Cleveland, Tennessee, p. 19.

important, you will be adopted into the family of God
with all the rights of sonship. R. H. Gause says, "As
the Spirit of adoption, He brings to us the knowledge
that we are the children of God. He assures us of this
by various methods; one of the most positive ways is
His leadership. 'For as many as are led by the Spirit of
God, they are the sons of God' (Rom. 8:14). This is
more stable than a mere emotional assurance of sonship."[32]

The who, what and where of regeneration can be noted
as: (1) the Spirit is the Agent, (2) the Word is the instrument and (3) the Cross is the place. I wonder if we
have dishonored the Spirit of God by trying to confine
His marvelous life-giving ministries to only one facet
of our faith. Have we hindered the free flowing of the
"living water" (John 7:37-39) by damming it up in one
little preconceived corner? M. G. McLuhan says,

> Many are quite unmindful of the Spirit's work in their
> lives prior to the Pentecostal enduement with power.
> Regeneration is the sole work of the Holy Ghost. The
> Holy Ghost alone can make true converts. He alone
> can regenerate men when they come to Him in re-
> pentance and faith. His works are: (a) Baptism into
> the Body of Christ (1 Cor. 12:13); (b) Changing the
> Christian's body into His temple (1 Cor. 3:16, 17,
> 6:19, 20); (c) Becoming the Christian's inner wit-
> ness of the new birth (Rom. 8:14-16; 1 John 5:10),
> and (d) Indwelling the heart of the Christian (Rom.
> 5:1-5, 8:9; Gal. 4:6, 7; 1 John 3:24, 4:12-16,
> 5:10-12). Regeneration, sanctification and the baptism
> with the Holy Ghost are all experiences that the be-
> liever has with or in the Spirit.[33]

Dr. Donald Bowdle explains,

---

32 Gause, *Evangel*, December 10, 1956, p. 9.
33 McLuhan, *op. cit.*, Lecture II, p. 1.

It is vitally important to understand that every Christian possesses the Holy Spirit in regenerating measure (Rom. 8:9; 1 Cor. 6:19). This is not to assert that every Christian has been baptized with the Holy Spirit. Indwelling and infilling are two completely different experiences. Without the former, one cannot be a child of God at all; without the latter, one cannot be fully effective in His service.[34]

Dr. Ray H. Hughes adds,

It is not the contention of Pentecostal Christians that true believers do not have the Spirit, for the Bible plainly sets forth the Spirit as the agency of the new birth (John 3:8; Rom. 5:5, 8:9, 14; Gal. 4:6; Titus 3:5; 1 John 3:24, 4:13). There is a decided difference in the terms "born of the Spirit" and "baptized with the Holy Spirit." There is one Holy Ghost. but there are diversities of operation (1 Cor. 12:6).[35]

The Spirit is the *Agent* of the new birth. He alone can communicate life. The Spirit makes true in us what Christ has made true for us. As Christ brought to us the things of the Father, the Spirit brings to us the things of the Son. As J. D. Bright said, "It is by the Holy Ghost that we are born again (John 3:5). By the same process, at the same time, and by the same Spirit we are baptized into the body of Christ (1 Cor. 12:13)."[36]

That the Word is the *instrument* of conversion has been evident throughout these pages (John 5:39, 20:3; James 1:18; 1 Peter 1:23). Man's sinful nature and God's holiness demanded the cross as the *place* of redemption (Ezra 9:5; John 3:6; Titus 3:5; Heb. 12:14; 1 John 1:7, 9). Jesus used Moses' serpent in the wil-

---

34 Bowdle, *op. cit.*, pp. 18, 19.
35 Hughes, *op. cit.*, pp. 25, 26.
36 J. D. Bright, *The Baptism of the Holy Ghost*, Church of God Publishing House, Cleveland, Tennessee, pp. 12, 13.

derness to illustrate it (John 3:12-15). One believing look at Calvary still means life to all who are dead in trespasses and sins. Faith in the blood of Jesus Christ is necessary for the remission of sins.

Unlike Russian cosmonaut Yuri Gagarin who flew right through the heavens and said, "I did not see God"; Astronaut John Glenn was not looking for God while in his *Friendship Seven* because he had already found Him many years ago, and he said, "He lives in my heart." "There is no doubt about it," says Pastor Houk, "John is a born-again Christian."[37] L. O. Vaught declares, "There is only one answer for a sin-sick world and that is a new life for the individual wrought by the regenerating power of the Holy Spirit. Nothing short of spiritual renewal in Christ will enable the individual to 'break away from it all' and live the abundant life."[38]

"In Sanctification"

Article six of the Church of God Declaration of Faith states, "We believe . . . In sanctification subsequent to the new birth, through faith in the blood of Christ; through the Word, and by the Holy Ghost" *(Minutes)*. In relating this experience by the Holy Ghost, we should understand its essence, its relationship to the cross, the Word and how it is subsequent. We will therefore consider the Sanctifying Spirit, the Sacrificing Spirit and the Sequential Spirit.

As the *sanctifying* Spirit, He is the Spirit of Holiness. Holiness, sanctification and consecration are generally

---

37 *Church of God Evangel,* "John Glenn Described as Born-again Christian," E. P. Special, April 23, 1962, p. 15.
38 L. O. Vaught, "God's Message for You: A New Life," *Evangel,* May 19, 1969, p. 14.

considered synonymous. The basic meaning is separation *from* and separation *unto*. Research will show that the strongest sense is not separation from that which is common or profane, but rather separation unto that which is sacred or for holy use. To be sure, the negative aspect is there, but it is referred to only in case it is needed. The weight of emphasis and meaning is positive, toward that which is Godlike or Christlike, where the negative is presupposed or taken for granted.*

> The Christian must remember that holiness is (1) to be like God in character and purpose (1 Peter 1:15, 16; 2 Peter 1:3-7; 1 John 2:6), (2) to be pure in thought, word and deed (Rom. 12:1-3; Phil. 4:8; James 3:17; 1 John 3:3), (3) to be blameless in spirit, soul and body (1 Thess. 5:23), (4) to be at peace with all men (Heb. 12:14), (5) to be a fruit-bearing Christian (Gal. 5:22, 23). This is the most dependable proof of real sanctification. A Christian who does not manifest love, joy, peace, longsuffering, gentleness, etc., is certainly not a holiness Christian.[39]

Dr. Ray H. Hughes emphasizes,

> Holiness in the sense of a definite decision of separation is a crisis experience. But holiness in the sense of conformity to Christ is a process. This crisis must take place before we can know the process. . . . It rests not in human measurements but in Christ. It is not acquired through abstinence but through faith in the blood of Christ—through the Word and by the Holy Ghost.[40]

The essence of holiness is Christlikeness. Jesus said, "They are not of the world, even as I am not of the world" (John 17:16). Their source was the same as

---

* For further study the reader is referred to Chapter One under "Holy."
39 M. G. McLuhan, "The Holy Spirit's Work in Regeneration and Sanctification," Lecture II, pp. 2, 3.
40 Hughes, *op. cit.*, p. 134.

Christ's (John 17:18, 20:21). The character of likeness follows throughout the whole scheme. Cleo Watts states,

> The law of the Spirit of life in Christ Jesus is the law of conformity to type. Life begins as raw protoplasm that looks the same under a microscope in all flesh, but within, there is a difference. The kind of life in the protoplasm determines the type of life to be developed. The devil within a man will produce the characteristics of the devil. The Holy Ghost within a man's life will produce the characteristics of God.[41]

The Holy Spirit is the *Agent* in sanctification (Rom. 15:16). As the Spirit of holiness (Rom. 1:4), He produces holiness and makes the holiness of God to be ours individually (Eph. 4:6). He is the Fountainhead of holiness. He is the Author of any longing which we have in our hearts after holiness. He is that Agency of transformation (changing from) and transfiguration (changing unto), who works a metamorphosis of character and conduct (outward change from within) in the believer.

He is the *sacrificing* Spirit. Not once did He abandon the Son in the redemptive mission. Without the cross there would be no redemption (Heb. 9:22). God's holiness demanded the cross. The drama is heightened when the universe becomes a temple, the cross the altar, and Christ, both priest and sacrifice, offers Himself without spot to God through the Eternal Spirit (Heb. 9:13, 14). Now the means of sanctification are available through faith in the blood of Jesus Christ (Heb. 10:10, 14, 13:12; 1 Cor. 1:30).

Our Lord gave the *instrument* of sanctification when He said, "Sanctify them through thy truth: thy word

---

41 Cleo Watts, "The Spirit Life," *Church of God Evangel*, Nov. 18, 1963, Cleveland, Tennessee, p. 13.

is truth" (John 17:17). Through the Word, the Spirit of truth brings sanctification to individuals (John 15:3, 17:14, 17, 19), to the church (Eph. 5:25-27; 1 Thess. 4:3; 2 Thess. 2:13), and to the world (John 17:20). The Agent of sanctification is the Holy Spirit—the Spirit of holiness; the instrument is the Word—the Spirit of truth; the element is the blood of Jesus Christ through the Eternal Spirit (Heb. 9:13, 14) and the place again is Calvary.

The *sequential* work of the Holy Spirit is as beautiful as the eternal continuity of His life-giving ministries. As the cosmos reveals His order, even so Biblical history is one unceasing flow of His action. Equally inspiring is His agency in human experience, teaching and guiding man through the successive steps of salvation and preparation for service. As conversion is subsequent to conviction, so sanctification is subsequent to regeneration. As the baptism of the Holy Ghost is subsequent to a clean heart, so power is subsequent to the baptism of the Holy Ghost (Acts 1:8).

"In Baptism"

Article eight of the Church of God Declaration of Faith states, "We believe . . . In the baptism with the Holy Ghost subsequent to a clean heart" *(Minutes)*. The baptism of the Holy Ghost has already been defined.* In this section it will be viewed from the standpoint of *design*—how it fits into the pattern of experience; *distinction*—how it is distinguished from other scriptural references to "baptism"; and *description*—a description of what symbolically takes place when a person receives the baptism in the Holy Spirit.

---

* See Chapter One under "The Baptism of the Holy Spirit."

Before a person is spiritually ready for the baptism in the Holy Ghost, he must be born again and set apart unto holiness (1 Thess. 4:7). Calvary always preceeds Pentecost. Sanctification subtracts by its cleansing, washing and purging process (Eph. 5:26; Heb. 9:13, 14). Baptism adds by its filling and overflowing process (Acts 2:4, 4:8, 31, 7:55, 9:17, 13:9, 52; Eph. 5:18). Before the Spirit will come into a heart, He must find one that is congenial to His nature. Holiness is a prerequisite to Pentecost. Does this mean that there is no growth in the Christian life? Absolutely not, there is a difference between purity and maturity. Making the heart pure is God's work, growing is a result of our own response to the light and opportunities we have in God (Eph. 4:12-15; 1 Peter 2:2; 2 Peter 3:18).

The contemporary student of the Holy Spirit should be able to distinguish between the numerous baptisms mentioned in the Scripture. This is especially true since the Pentecostal experience is referred to as the baptism of the Holy Ghost (Matt. 3:11; Acts 1:5). Those who would deny this experience often try to confuse it with one or more of the other baptisms. Two things must be understood: (1) the Word of God speaks of several baptisms and (2) the context must be considered carefully in order to determine what is meant. We will distinguish between (a) all baptisms, (b) believer's baptisms and (c) the baptism in the Holy Spirit.

There are seven baptisms referred to in the Scripture: 1. Moses' baptism in the cloud and in the sea (Ex. 14:19-21; 1 Cor. 10:1, 2); 2. John's baptism in water (Matt. 3:6; John 1:31-33; Acts 19:3); 3. Christ's baptism in water (John 3:22; 4:1, 2); 4. Baptism in suffering (Luke 12:50); 5. Christian baptism in water

(Matt. 28:19; Acts 2:38-41; 1 Peter 3:21); 6. Baptism into Christ and into the body (Rom. 6:3, 4; 1 Cor. 12:13; Gal. 3:27; Eph. 4:5; Col. 2:12); 7. Baptism in the Holy Spirit (Matt. 3:11; Acts 1:5; 11:16).

There are three basic baptisms for believers. 1. The baptism into Christ or into His body at repentance and the new birth. This is the "one baptism" (1 Cor. 12:13; Eph. 4:5) and the only baptism that saves. It refers to the unity of the body of Christ and there is but one baptism into His body. 2. Water baptism was commanded by our Lord. This mode of baptism is by immersion. The baptismal formula is "in the name of the Father, and of the Son, and of the Holy Ghost." All who repent should follow the example of Christ in water baptism. It is not a means of regeneration, but dramatizes the work of regeneration in the life of the believer. 3. The baptism of the Holy Ghost with the enduement of power for service is a baptism as received on the Day of Pentecost (Acts 2:4). It can be either a pre-immersion (Acts 10:44-48) or a post-immersion experience (Acts 8:14-17).

There are three things to understand in a proper baptism. 1. The *Agent* is the one baptizing or administering baptism. 2. The *Element* is that in which one is to be baptized. 3. The *Candidate* is the one receiving the baptism experience. In the baptism into Christ and His body, the Holy Spirit is the Agent, Christ and His body is the Element and the believer is the candidate. In water baptism the minister is the agent, water is the element and the believer is the candidate. In the Spirit baptism, Christ is the Agent, the Holy Spirit is the Element and the believer is the candidate. The element into which one is baptized determines the kind of baptism one has experienced.

There are many expressions of the Spirit's action spoken of in the Scriptures. The most common are, having the Spirit in, within, upon, or being filled and moved by the Spirit. The most common portions of the Spirit mentioned are the Mosaic portion which was divided seventy-one ways (Num. 11:16, 17, 25-29), and Elijah's portion—John the Baptist's measure, which was doubled to Elisha (Luke 1:15-17; 2 Kings 2:9, 10). The words "measure, portion or proportion" do not refer to baptism for it is given "without measure" (John 3:34).

Numerous object lessons have been used to illustrate the difference between "a filling" and "a baptism," or one's receiving the Spirit "by measure" and "without measure." One method is the use of a small glass and a large tumbler of water. By submerging the smaller into the larger tumbler of water it is both filled and baptized. A filling always comes with a baptism, but a baptism does not always come with a filling. At Pentecost they were both filled and baptized (Acts 1:4, 5; 2:4).

James L. Slay sets the stage by asking, "What could possibly be better than living in the presence of the only begotten Son of the Father? The coming of the Spirit at Pentecost erased all doubt. . . . Pentecost transcended this sense of His presence: It was something corresponding to the difference between 'with-ness and in-ness' (John 14:17)."[42]

C. R. Spain opens the curtain,

> The hour has come and the High Priest in the Temple is waving two loaves before God. The Hebrews are at the height of ecstatic expectation. At the precise

---

42 James L. Slay, "Pentecostal Experience—Its Value to the Individual," *Church of God Evangel*, Cleveland, Tennessee, May 27, 1968, p. 13.

moment as the Priest lifts the wave offering, the cloud of glory bursts forth upon the 120 like a gushing whirlwind from heaven. They are thrilled with indescribable glory. Tongues, like as fire, are sitting upon each one, and they are speaking languages they have not learned and do not understand. While their shouts of praise roll out upon the streets, Hebrews come running representing the world—from Parthia in the east—to Italy in the west, and from the Euxine (Black) Sea in the north to Egypt in the south. Each hears the gospel in the language of his country, spoken by the unlearned Galileans. The disciples had been baptized in the Holy Ghost.[43]

Knowing that *baptism* means "yielding to the skill of the Baptizer and accepting the power of the Element," the candidate presents himself to Christ at the place of baptism. He acknowledges that baptism does not depend upon what he can do, but upon what Christ can do for him. Walking in the Spirit, he submits himself into the hands of Christ who places and submerges him in the Holy Spirit. He is literally inundated, deluged, flooded and saturated in the Spirit. There is no part of him left out. His total self, the physical, the mental and the emotional—every phase of his life is engulfed with God. Quickened and ignited by the Spirit's fire, he rises speaking in tongues and filled with power to emulate Christ in attitude, in action and in mission. God is in that man, for He has filled Him with Himself, baptizing him with the Holy Ghost and with fire.

"In Power"

A young lady rushed to tell her pastor that she had just received the baptism of the Holy Ghost. The pastor

---

43 C. R. Spain, "The Baptism of the Holy Ghost," *Church of God Evangel,* May 28, 1962, Cleveland, Tennessee, p. 7.

rejoiced with her briefly and then quietly asked, "And for what purpose? Why did you receive your Baptism?" This is the point toward which the Holy Spirit has been leading us. His work in revelation, conviction, conversion, sanctification and baptism is now at stake. The result of the application is the proof of the pudding. *Dunamis* is the ability to do something.* When it is God's *dunamis,* it is not power to do what we want, but power to do what God has commissioned. The baptism is defined by Peter as "this is that" (Acts 2:16). This power is described by Christ as "after that." Did He mean that the full proof of a real Pentecost comes "after that" —we leave the altar, leave the company of the committed and encounter an opportunity to tell someone? Pentecost is a power baptism. *Glossolalia* is its initial evidence, but power to witness is its essence. This is the same kind of power which God has and must be exerted in the same mission as His Great Commission (Matt. 28:19; John 20:21).

The *action* to which this power must be applied is *witnessing.* The purpose and point of Pentecostal power is, "Ye shall be witnesses." To witness implies three things: (1) To remember, which means to give information, bring to light and confirm; (2) To assert, meaning to support your statements on the strength of your own experience or authority; (3) To be a martyr, or to bear witness to the truth by death.[44] In reality we are always witnessing, either for or against. Witnessing for Christ is the universal obligation of all Christians (Luke 24:48; Acts 1:8). This is one of the most needed emphases of the twentieth century church. We are to be witnesses without regard for safety or comfort. Power

---

* See Chapter One under "Power."
44 Bullinger, *op. cit.,* p. 893.

and witnessing are as interrelated as power and the Holy
Spirit.

In his book *Saved to Serve* Donald Aultman reveals,
"A prominent college published in a statistical report
that ninety-five percent of all Christians have never
brought a sinner to Jesus Christ for salvation.[45]

Assigning a lack of witnessing to know-how, Paul
Henson recommends,

> Read and study closely the method of Christ and
> Phillip in chapter four of St. John and chapter eight
> of the Acts of the Apostles, then follow these four
> suggestions. 1. Be available to the Holy Spirit anywhere,
> anytime. 2. Endeavor to arouse an interest in spiritual
> things in those with whom you come in contact.
> 3. Study and learn the Word of God. 4. Keep your
> witness Christ-centered, and avoid becoming a crutch
> to those with whom you share your faith.[46]

Aubrey Maye advises, "Your goal is to present the simple
Bible plan of salvation so as to bring (1) conviction
of sin, (2) repentance, and (3) faith in Christ as Saviour. Mark these Scriptures in your Bible and use them
(Luke 13:3; John 1:12, 3:16; Rom. 3:23, 6:23, 10:9;
Titus 3:5; 1 John 1:9)."[47] Carl Richardson says, "The
message of Jesus Christ is to be shared by those who
care. That is the way it spread in the Early Church.
Andrew brought Peter, and Philip brought Nathanael,
and down through the ages that is the way men have
been coming to Christ."[48] The problem is not that peo-

45 Donald S. Aultman, *Saved to Serve*, Sunday School and Youth Department, Cleveland, Tennessee, p. 5.

46 Paul F. Henson, "How to Share Your Christian Faith," *Campus Call*,
Jan.-Feb., 1969, pp. 12, 13.

47 Aubrey Maye, *Pentecostal Witnessing*, Pathway Press, Cleveland,
Tenn., pp. 51, 63.

48 Carl Richardson, *Let's Have Revival*, Pathway Press, Cleveland, Tenn.,
1969, p. 15.

ple won't listen, but that the Christians won't tell. The power of the Holy Spirit must be applied to the action of witnessing.

The *reflection* of that witness must be Jesus Christ. The prophets and John the Baptist pointed men to Christ (Isa. 7:14; John 1:29, 36, 3:30). Jesus said, "Ye shall be . . . unto me" (Acts 1:8). A Spirit anointed witness will point men to the Lamb of God (John 12:32). No man can bear witness to himself and Christ at the same time. No man can give the impression that he himself is clever and that Christ is mighty to save. The cry of the lost is, "Sirs, we would see Jesus." Dave Wilkerson declares, "There is only one ultimate solution to life and all its problems and that is Jesus Christ. Go out and offer Christ as the ultimate solution."[49] Dr. Carl F. H. Henry says, "Everything men still need to have heaven on earth is to be found in Jesus Christ and nowhere else."[50]

While much is said about the impact of the direct witness, we must not underestimate the effective indirect encounters that reflect Christ. What we are, is as vocal as what we say. The convictions we hold, the attitudes we display, the high sense of duty by which we are moved, the thousand little acts of every work-a-day week —these make us magnets by which people are drawn to our Saviour. Dr. Delton L. Alford says, "Today's youth need and deserve to be exposed to an everyday, consistent, practical expression of those words which they hear expounded by adults in the pulpits, lived out in the classroom and at home."[51]

---

49 David Wilkerson, "Youth In Rebellion," *Church of God Evangel,* November 10, 1969, Cleveland, Tenn., p. 16.

50 Carl F. H. Henry, "World Evangelism or World Revolution," *Church of God Evangel,* July 25, 1966, Cleveland, Tennessee, p. 7.

51 "Campus Unrest and the Church," *Church of God Evangel,* July 7, 1969, p. 4.

The *direction* of our witness is *"both* in Jerusalem, and all Judaea, and in Samaria, *and* unto the uttermost part of the earth." Christianity is designed for the road as well as the sanctuary. If Satan can confine this message to our four walls, we are defeated. This message must not be contained. It is designed to overflow, pour out and leap man-made boundaries and barriers, cultures and sub-cultures, races and religions—and possess the hearts that are hungry for God. The church needs a new sense of purpose. We need to rediscover the nature and mission of the New Testament Church. Why are we here? When we lose our purpose for existing, we are in danger of losing our existence. The contemporary situation is and always has been a missionary situation. Pentecost and missions are inseparable. Missions was not so in the Early Church and is not today an overseas project alone. Missions is the task of the church wherever it finds itself. Jesus said to witness in the inner city, the suburbs, the off-limits, and to the ends of the earth. Dave Wilkerson says, "It's a lot easier to love the world than your neighbor. We need to change the question 'Am I my brother's keeper?' to the statement 'I am my brother's keeper.' "

Heinrich Scherz writes of the "vertical slums" in the inner city.

> Old churches with boarded windows and padlocked doors give mute testimony to the flight of the churches to the suburbs. Yet there are those who have been called by Christ and are under orders to bring hope to these in need. Once we are identified with Christ we have no choice but to accept, as our own, Christ's mission to preach the gospel to the poor (Luke 4:18).[52]

---

[52] Heinrich C. Scherz, "Adrift in the City," *Church of God Evangel*, August 4, 1969, pp. 3, 4.

In his guest editorial Wade H. Horton asks, "Are we ready to abandon any segment of our society as unreachable?"

> During my recent detainment in New York City, I watched these extremely different young people. Their faces and their eyes revealed something to me I had never seen before. I saw a sad lostness, an endless searching for answers that have puzzled the minds of men from the beginning. These young people are lost, both to society and to God. Nevertheless, they do need God; they desperately need God. When are we going to graduate from our catechisms and kindergartens? When will our members be promoted from "sanctuary saints" to "sidewalk saints"? When will we leave our "Haven of Rest" and go out into the "harvest fields" of Highways and Hedges Evangelism? We say we have a whole gospel for the whole man in the whole world. Here is a chance to prove it. If we have the answer, we also have the responsibility.[53]

Former missionary Dr. James M. Beaty says,

> In Chile the Pentecostals took to the streets to preach and witness to Christ. Today nine out of ten Protestants are Pentecostal. The movement is even larger in Brazil where Spirit-filled laymen are moved to take Christ to the lost. The church can only fulfill its purpose in the world through the indwelling presence and power of the Holy Spirit. Clothed in this power, "the gates of hell shall not prevail against it."[54]

> > Breathe on me, Breath of God,
> > Fill me with life anew;
> > That I may love what thou dost love,
> > And do what thou wouldst do.

53 Wade H. Horton, "Marked Off—Rejected," *Church of God Evangel,* November 10, 1969, pp. 3, 4.
54 James M. Beaty, "The Holy Spirit—His Presence and Power in the Church," *Church of God Evangel,* May 19, 1969, p. 11.

3

The Holy Spirit in Demonstration

(The Gifts of the Spirit)

In Church of God Teachings, number ten refers to "Spiritual gifts (1 Cor. 12:1, 7, 10, 28, 31; 14:1)"— *Minutes.* Since a forthcoming study, (CTC 306), will deal exclusively with "the gifts of the Spirit," it will be the purpose of this chapter to give only a brief survey of the subject. The use of the word "demonstration" with the gifts and "manifestation" with the fruit is simply one of choice. The words are practically synonymous and can be used interchangeably (1 Cor. 12:7). Demonstration is used in the sense that it shows, points out and proves by a public display or demonstration (1 Cor. 2:4). We will deal with (1) the Donor or source, (2) the Dispenser or the distributor, (3) the difference in each individual gift, (4) the dimension or sphere of operation, (5) the danger, abuse, or misuse of the gifts and (6) the decision or evaluation of gifts versus fruit.

God is seen as the prime Donor (John 14:16, 26;

15:26, 16:7; Luke 11:13; Acts 5:32). The gifts are inseparably linked with the Gift. Their services, ministries and workings are all evidence of God the Father, God the Son, and God the Holy Spirit (1 Cor. 12:4-6). The giving of gifts is God's business. He is the fountain of all gifts (Eph. 4:10; James 1:17). The gifts are the *charismata.** Two words used by Paul are *charismata* and *pneumatika.* The former refers to that which has its source in the grace of God (Rom. 12:6; 1 Cor. 12:4). The latter shows the relationship to the Spirit *(pneuma),* meaning that they are given through and are controlled by the Spirit of God (1 Cor. 12:4, 7, 11). Dr. R. Leonard Carroll says, "The triune God of His own will is the giver and controller of the gifts. They operate not at the command of man, but in accordance with the power of God who controls and directs the miracle."[1] Dr. Charles W. Conn says, "God holds the power of the gifts within Himself. He retains control."[2]

These gifts, spirituals or enablements are dispensed by the Holy Spirit (1 Cor. 12:11). They are not natural talents. They are neither purchased, merited or deserved. They are disbursed freely by the Spirit, "to everyman . . . as he will." All references of chapter twelve to *diversities, differences* and *dividing* are from a root word meaning "to take asunder, to divide into parts and to distribute."[3] The repetition of the plural forms suggest repeated distributions by the one and same Spirit. The division is both inclusive and selective. It is "to every man," yet as He wills (1 Cor. 12:7-11). Sam Shoemaker says,

---

* See Chapter One under "Charismatic Endowment."
1 Horton, *Glossolalia Phenomenon, op. cit.,* p. 90.
2 Charles W. Conn, "The Dynamics of Spiritual Gifts," *Church of God Evangel,* March 5, 1962, p. 4.
3 Vine, *op. cit.,* pp. 310, 327.

"Don't rule yourself out—there is no exclusion except those who exclude themselves. . . . Even God can't include them. Let yourself go into the hands of God. Pray not for your own satisfaction, but for His glory and for the needs of people about you—then let things begin to happen, till the Holy Spirit wears a channel through you."[4]

Ray H. Hughes says, "All of the spiritual gifts are resident in the Holy Ghost, and when one is full of the Holy Ghost, he has the potential of all the spiritual gifts."[5] While the division and choice is wrought by the initiative and sole prerogative of the Spirit, the believer is enjoined to "covet earnestly the best gifts." Don't try to dictate to the Spirit but put yourself at His disposal. "Quench not the Spirit" (1 Thess. 5:19), but rather allow Him to energize and use you any time and anywhere, as He desires.

There are several catalogs of gifts, offices and ministries of the Spirit listed in the New Testament (Rom. 12:3-8; 1 Cor. 12:8-10; 28-30; Eph. 4:7-11). Even in the Old Testament there is the energizing and the super-adding of the Spirit to aid man in accomplishing the work of God. We will discuss the difference in the nine which are identified in 1 Cor. 12:8-10.

1. The Word of Wisdom. Bullinger calls it "a right application of knowledge." Vine defines it as "insight into the true nature of things." Ralph Riggs says, "Wisdom is knowledge rightly applied. Wisdom builds with the materials which knowledge provides. It is discreet action on the basis of knowledge. Its objective is to

---

4 Samuel Shoemaker, "Charismatic People," *Christian Life* (Dec. 1963), Vol. 25, p. 33.

5 Hughes, *op. cit.,* p. 47.

bring to pass ends which will glorify God."[6] Not only the ends, but also the means will glorify God. Man is only a channel or a vehicle. God is the source. The demonstration of the word of wisdom is not the exercise of natural skill alone, but is the super-adding of God to that which already exists, and if necessary, is a complete endowment in order to accomplish the will of God. McLuhan says,

> This means divinely imparted intelligence and the practical action that goes with it. It is first manifested in the spoken word and then demonstrated in everyday living (1 Cor. 2:5-7, 13). It is essential in every phase of Christian life and service (James 1:5). It holds the same place in the order of "spirituals," as love holds in the order of spiritual fruit (1 Cor. 12:8; Gal. 5:22).[7]

Donald Gee says, "The Word of Wisdom is the teaching of the deep things of God which the Spirit alone can search out and reveal."[8]

2. *The Word of Knowledge.* Goodspeed calls this the power to express knowledge; Beck, the ability to speak intelligently; Taylor, especially good at study, and Jordan, a keen mind. Riggs suggests knowledge as a prerequisite to both wisdom and teaching. As a gift from God it suggests accessibility to those things of which the omniscient God is the source, such as is reflected in life, the universe, the Gospels and the Pauline Epistles (John 21:17; Rom. 15:14; 2 Cor. 2:14, 10:5; Col. 2:3). The reference to "the word of" knowledge and wisdom

---

6 Ralph M. Riggs, *The Spirit Himself*, Gospel Publishing House, Springfield, Mo., 1949, pp. 121, 127. Used by permission.

7 M. G. McLuhan, "The Spirituals or Charismatic Endowments," Lecture IV, p. 3.

8 Donald Gee, *Spiritual Gifts*, Gospel Publishing House, Springfield, Mo., 1963, p. 25. Used by permission.

is from *logos*. Jesus was the living *logos* (John 1:1) and the Bible is the written *logos*. The exercise of these enablements are not wisdom and knowledge alone, but that which reflects the wisdom and knowledge of God in Christ. It infers a constant process of growth (Eph. 4:15; 1 Peter 2:2; 2 Peter 3:18). McLuhan suggests the gift is not imparted to take the place of study or to encourage carelessness and laziness in the study of the Word of God. It is that spiritual knowledge which imparts true meaning to the Word as it is sincerely studied.

3. *Faith*. This is the same power by which God speaks and things come to pass. It suggests a close relationship to God and His Word (John 15:7). It is the greatest of the gifts of power (Heb. 11:3). It is distinguished from saving faith and the fruit of the Spirit (Heb. 11:6; Gal. 5:22). It is a holy certainty that triumphs over everything. The literal translation "Have the faith of God" (Mark 11:22) gives us a hint as to the quality of this endowment. It is that mountain moving attribute of God dropped into the soul of man to aid him in accomplishing these and "greater . . . than these" acts (Matt. 17:20; John 14:12). Faith is a matter of the Christian's relationship with God from start to finish (Rom. 1:17). It is that through which all the gifts are demonstrated, and without which it is impossible to please God (Heb. 11:6).

4. *Gifts of Healing*. This denotes "gifts of healings" where both nouns are plural, indicating healing powers for as many sicknesses as there are varieties of diseases. This endowment is exercised to minister health to the sick and afflicted through prayer (Acts 8:6, 7). All believers in general, and elders in particular, are empowered to pray for the sick (Mark 16:18; James 5:14). This is

probably the most frequently exercised gift. Three words in the Greek New Testament refer to healing: (1) *therapeia* meaning the care and attention of one who serves the sick; (2) *iama* meaning the complete act of healing; and (3) *iasis* referring to a process unto healing.

The gifts of healings are recorded by the use of number two and means the divine healing that takes place apart from the aid of natural means or human skills. It does not deny or denounce other means, it only announces the privilege of the believer. The Church of God believes that divine healing is provided for all in the Atonement (Ex. 15:26; Psa. 103:3; Isa. 53:5, 6; 1 Peter 2:24).[9] This refers primarily to physical infirmity, but can refer to body, soul and spirit (John 7:23). While healing is a privilege provided for all, not all are healed as was indicated in Christ's ministry (Matt. 13:58).

5. *The Working of Miracles.* This means the "workings of powers" or the "energies of powers." This does not mean healings, as these are separate gifts. The miraculous refers to God breaking in—an orderly intervention into the regular operation of nature. Vine calls it a work of supernatural origin or character, such as could not be produced by natural agents or means.[10]

J. B. Phillips calls it the power to do great deeds. It is that special authentication that accompanies the believer who dramatizes Christ to this world (Acts 6:8). The Church of God teaches that signs will follow believers (Mark 16:17-20; Rom. 15:18, 19; Heb. 2:4). It does not teach that believers should follow signs.

6. *Prophecy.* More than to foretell, the gift of prophecy

---

9 *Minutes, op. cit.,* p. 4.
10 Vine, *op. cit.,* Vol. III, p. 75.

is Divine ability to tell forth the whole counsel of God. Goodspeed calls it inspiration in preaching; Phillips— the gift of preaching the Word of God; Wuest—the giving forth of divine relations and *Good News for Modern Man* translates it "the gift of speaking God's message." It means to speak for another in one's own language in the power of the Spirit. It expresses and conveys the emotions of God. Revelation expresses His mind, power expresses His omnipotence, and prophetic utterance expresses His heart. A true prophet is a man with a message from God who interprets His divine will and purpose in inspired preaching and teaching. Preaching and teaching is a product of studying the existing revelation. Prophecy is a result of spontaneous inspiration—not intended to replace preaching and teaching but to supplement and reinforce it with the fresh touch of God. This makes the difference in our Pentecostal witness and aids us in reaching man for God. "The man who prophesies is talking to men and his words have power to build; they stimulate and they encourage" (1 Cor. 14:3, *New English Bible*).

7. *Discerning of Spirits.* This is power to discriminate in spiritual matters (Phillips); to distinguish between true and false inspiration *(Twentieth Century Encyclopedia);* a correct evaluation of individuals who give forth divine revelations (Wuest); a sensitive spiritual insight (Jordan); and the ability to tell the difference between gifts that come from the Spirit and those that do not *(Good News for Modern Man)*. It enables one to see through all outward appearances, to know one's true nature (John 1:47-50, 3:1-3), and to unmask an enemy in disguise (Acts 5:1-11, 8:23, 13:6-12, 16:16-18).

There are three tests which can be applied: one, loyalty to Christ (Matt. 16:16, 17; 1 Cor. 12:3); two, the doctrinal test (1 John 4:1-6); and three, the practical test (Matt. 7:15-23).[11] The gift of discernment should be distinguished from acquired skills which understand and predict human behavior. It should especially be distinguished from those who persist in fault finding. It relates solely to the discernment of true spiritual character.

8. *Divers Kinds of Tongues.* The gift of tongues is not the same as the initial evidence.* All recipients do not receive the gift of tongues. All who have received the gift *(doran)* have the potential of receiving the gifts *(charismata)*. The initial evidence is an "in the beginning" sign of receiving the gift *(doran)*. The exercise of divers kinds of tongues is one demonstration of the gifts *(charismata)* dispensed by the Spirit severally "as he wills." The Scriptures are very clear as to the proper exercise of glossolalia (1 Cor. 14:13-28). Dr. Charles W. Conn says, "The initial evidence is distinct from the gift of tongues. Spiritual gifts generally follow rather than accompany the Holy Spirit baptism."[12]

This gift is referred to as the ability to talk strange languages (Beck); various ecstatic utterances (Goodspeed); a catalog of tongues (Jordan); the ability to speak with strange sounds (Good News); and the supernatural utterance in other languages which are not known to the speaker (Dake). Dr. Conn explains the nature of tongues,

> When the disciples first spoke in tongues it was in clear, precise, understandable languages. The speaking

---

11 Pearlman, *op. cit.,* pp. 332-334.
* See Chapter One under "Initial Evidence."
12 Conn, *Pillars of Pentecost, op. cit.,* p. 35.

was not in unintelligible gibberish, but the speakers
spoke words and sentences of proper grammatical struc-
ture; whose syntax was accurate and whose passages
were connected. God has not yet stooped to repetitious
and meaningless banality. Gibberish is not the language
of the Spirit. When the Spirit speaks. . . . it will not
be in dead, pompous, monotonous, or pointless ver-
biage. . . . it will be exalted praise for convicting exhortation. . . . it will be in phrases as exalted and
errorless as the language of the Bible, for He is the
Author or it, too.[13]

9. *Interpretation of Tongues.* This is an accompanying gift of tongues. It is supernatural, entirely dependent
upon the gift of tongues and has no function apart from
it. It has nothing to do with the interpretation of Scripture. It is the ability to interpret the meaning of a message given in an unknown tongue. It is that which makes
the unknown to become known. It does not necessarily
imply a word for word translation, commentary or gist.
It is rendering the sense, the significance and the explanation of a message in an understandable and com-
prehensive vernacular. It is an important gift. Speaking
in tongues accompanied by the interpretation of tongues
or in prayer, praise and personal edification, within the
scriptural context is definitely in order (1 Cor. 14:5-13,
16-20, 23, 27, 28). If there is no interpreter when
the gift of tongues is exercised, the speaker should pray
that he might interpret, and if not, should keep silent
or speak to himself.

The purpose for tongues is to speak to God (1 Cor.
14:2); the purpose for prophecy is to speak to man.
Tongues accompanied with interpretation is equal to
prophecy (1 Cor. 14:5) and should have the same ef-

---

13 *Ibid.,* p. 57.

fect (1 Cor. 12:7; 14:22). Why not prophecy rather than tongues and interpretations? Keep in mind that it is God's idea and is a sign to the unbeliever (1 Cor. 14:22). When one reflects upon the glossolalia phenomenon, the gift of divers kinds of tongues and interpretation of tongues, he can thank God for the means to express the inexpressible (1 Peter 1:8). As Charles Wesley exclaimed,

> O for a thousand tongues to sing, My great Redeemer's praise:
> The glories of my God and King, the triumphs of His grace.[14]

The dimension of the gifts refers to the scriptural sphere of their operation. The gifts are designed for the church (1 Cor. 12:28). Dr. Charles Conn says, "To be sure, the gifts are set in the church."[15] "Gifts are not for personal aggrandizement, but are to 'profit withal.' They profit the church not the individual."[16] The gifts are for edification, exhortation and comfort of the church (1 Cor. 14:12). The chief end of the charismata is to build up, promote spiritual growth and to develop character (1 Cor. 14:4, 5, 17, 26, 40). It is a continuous and progressive action.

This edifying dimension is also balanced and unified. Dr. A. W. Tozer says,

> A proper understanding of the gifts of the Spirit in the Church must depend upon a right concept of the nature of the Church. In three of his Epistles, Paul sets forth Christ as the Head of the Church which is His body. As a normal body consists of various obedient

---

14 Charles Wesley, *Hymns of the Spirit*, Pathway Press, Cleveland, Tenn., 1969, p. 19.
15 Conn, "The Dynamics of Spiritual Gifts," *op. cit.*
16 McLuhan, *op. cit.*, p. 2.

members with a head to direct them, so the true
Church is a body. The intelligent head can work only
as it has at its command organs designed for various
tasks. It is the mind that sees, but it must have an
eye to see through, and likewise, it cannot hear without
an ear. So the work of the church is done by members
with specifically created abilities through which the
Spirit can flow toward ordained ends.[17]

The body is related cooperatively, organically and
sympathetically. There are various parts, but one body.
All are engaged in vital functions toward a common
end. There are as many tasks as there are members.
There is no member without a ministry, for the body
of Christ must not have any useless members. "The gifts
operate in answer to a need and not as religious exercises in the field of spiritual phenomena. They are intended to work together in harmony. God expects all of
them to be operating in the church. If only one or two
are in evidence, the atmosphere is not what the New
Testament indicates it should be."[18]

The Gifts are valueless unless exercised within the
dimension of love. It was no accident that the great
love chapter appears in the center of Paul's discussion
on the gifts. The chapter is not only about love, it is
about the gifts. Giving is the action of love (John 3:16).
Spiritual gifts are tools for demonstrating love. The gifts
are necessary for this manifestation and love is necessary
for the proper use of the gifts. The first three verses of
chapter thirteen are very emphatic on one thing (1 Cor.
13:1-3). Gifts present and operating, outside the dimension of love, are no more than a hollow-sounding horn

---

17 A. W. Tozer, "Are They for Us Today," *Christian Life*, Oct., 1957,
pp. 24, 25.
18 McLuhan, *op. cit.*

or a nerve-wracking rattle (Jordan). The word "nothing" refers to "not one thing, not even one." The word is prefixed with an unconditional negative that is absolute, direct and without exception. It actually implies "I have already become and at present am nonexistent."[19] The gifts must be demonstrated in an atmosphere that manifests the fruit of the Spirit.

While the gifts are set in the church, the church is made up of individuals. Operating through imperfect vehicles the gifts are subject to frequent misuse. This was the reason for the gift of discernment, for John's admonition (1 John 4:1) and for Paul's advice to Thessalonica (1 Thess. 5:21). Because of these weaknesses, Paul had no choice but to establish rules of control over spiritual gifts and declare the need for subjection to them (1 Cor. 14:29-32). The contemporary scene requires that we consider the dangers inherent in the overuse of certain gifts, their abuse and the disuse of others.

The problem in Corinth was their overemphasis on speaking in tongues. Paul did not recommend repression (1 Cor. 14:39), but rather taught them spiritual discipline. He points out the dangers as well as the benefits in this marvelous power. He calls their attention away from a self-centered egotism to the Christ-centered good of the whole body. Their problem was an imbalance in the body by an overemphasis on the spectacular gifts. Man, with his feet of clay, always gets into trouble when he takes the things of God into his own hands (Matt. 23:23). Any imbalance or overemphasis fosters extremes. One extreme provokes its opposite. Over formalism tempts one to flee toward fanatical zeal, and frenzied zeal

---

19 Bullinger, *op. cit.,* pp. 525, 536.

tempts one to seek the peace and decency of some formalism. Truth is usually found somewhere between two extremes.

We should avoid extremes. They create a vacuum which produces all types of substitutes for the Spirit's power, such as imitation instead of inspiration and the worked up instead of the poured out. Reality is often crucified between the two extremes of formalism and fanaticism. A well-balanced Christian is a blessing wherever he goes. His influence and Christlike example will edify after he is gone. A well-balanced church is caught up in a spontaneous love for God, for their neighbor and for each other. Their services are characterized by praise for the presence of the Giver rather than His gifts. Maintaining such a balance is a continuous task, but beautiful, strengthening and life-giving wherever it is found.

The second danger is the abuse of the gifts. The word "deception" best characterizes the activities of Satan (Matt. 24:24; Rom. 16:18; 1 Cor. 3:18-23; 2 Tim. 3:13). Caution should be exercised in claiming exclusive personal possession of the gifts. There is danger in the church having to wait on the gifted few. The ability to exercise the gifts does not reside with man but with God. The Spirit in His Lordship will energize any obedient member. No one through whom a gift operates has anything or anyone in which to glory except God. "To God be the glory, great things He hath done." There is abuse in a narrow concept of what constitutes the supernatural. Such refuse to accept the better gifts as demonstrations of God's power. Beware of that which whispers, "He is not spiritual," or "That church is not spiritual." Such abuse existed in the New Testament (Matt. 7:21-24;

Luke 18:9-14; John 12:1-8; 1 Cor. 14:37, 38; Gal. 6:1).

The best way to test what is spiritual is to ask if it is scriptural. There is also abuse in pressuring and forcing the use of certain gifts. If there is no message in tongues and interpretation, some think the service is judged as dry or dead. There are those who think there must be messages in all services; for these are the only ones we exalt or talk about as being so wonderful. Donald Gee says, "Movements that make too much of messages through spiritual gifts inevitably sign their own death warrant. These things are never intended to be the hobby of little religious clubs. The burring flame of Pentecost is expressed in lifting up Christ as the Saviour of the world."[20] The gifts are further abused by refusing to obey the free and orderly flow of the Spirit (1 Thess. 5:19). They are abused by the opposite lack of control (1 Cor. 14:32) which brings confusion, disorder and oftentimes disgrace (1 Cor. 14:33, 40).

The answer is found in the Word of God. The disuse of the gifts can be traced to our failure in teaching their proper use. It takes courage to give, and humility to receive spiritual instructions on spiritual manifestations. Many find it convenient to avoid the subject because of a few unteachables. No church is worthy to exercise that in which it refuses to be instructed. It is like rushing to operate powerful and dangerous equipment prior to reading the manual of instructions. When you see the sign, "Dynamite," you also read the word, "Danger." The gifts are not playthings for inexperienced children (1 Cor. 14:20). Pandemonium often reigns because of

20 Donald Gee, "Blessing or Bathos," *Pentecostal Evangel*, Jan. 16, 1966, p. 4.

the lack of instruction and the damage is irreparable. He who touches power without proper instructions is endangering himself and the flock. Paul's chapter fourteen gives the controls by which the power is to be regulated, so that it will build rather than destroy.

None of these experiences are ends in themselves. They are gateways into deeper and fuller service to God. The decision, then, is not one of "gifts versus fruit" in the strictest sense. It is not an "either-or" decision, but rather one of priority. Dr. Conn says, "We cannot elevate and exalt spiritual gifts above simple mercy, simple grace and simple love. . . . We must beware lest we look at something akin to a gift and regard it as the distinguishing mark of Christianity. Divine love is the distinguishing mark for a child of God (John 13:35). . . . The gifts take no preeminence over Christian love."[21]

Dr. Bowdle says, "Know assuredly that the baptism in the Holy Spirit cannot legitimately be claimed prior to the washing of regeneration, nor can the gifts of the Spirit genuinely operate in the life that does not first bear His fruit."[22]

The New Testament gifts are as needed in our time as in the first century. Their scriptural function should characterize the normal ministry of a church to its community. The exercise of all the gifts should be the expected thing in all churches and should bring honor only to God. The contemporary ministry of the church is a body ministry, a balanced, healthy thrust of wholeness in the community. This is evident in our time.

---

21 Conn, *op. cit.*
22 Donald N. Bowdle, "Power for Service," *Church of God Evangel,* May 8, 1967, Cleveland, Tennessee, p. 7.

4

The Holy Spirit in Manifestation

(The Fruit of the Spirit)

Satan can imitate the gifts but not the fruit. "But the fruit of the Spirit is love, joy, peace, longsuffering, gentleness, goodness, faith, meekness, temperance: against such there is no law" (Gal. 5:22, 23). To manifest something is to make it evident to the senses, to exhibit or to display. A "manifesto" is an invoice of the ship's cargo, that which is to be exhibited and examined at the custom house (Matt. 7:16, 17).

"The Contrast"

There is a great contrast between the works of the flesh *(sarx)* and the fruit of the Spirit *(pneuma)* (Gal. 5:19-23). The flesh refers to human nature as weakened and tainted by sin; man, as he is apart from Jesus Christ and His Spirit (vv. 19-21). The flesh versus the Spirit pits the limitations of man against an illimitable Deity and the decay of the flesh versus the eternity of the Spirit. While Paul's list is not an exhaustive catalog, it does give us examples to review. Most commentaries divide the works of the flesh into four units. A basic list reads:

A. Sensual sins—misdirected physical desires

1. Adultery and fornication *(porneia)*, which means to prostitute or to sell. This refers to all unlawful and immoral sexual relationships between men and women, single or married, including incest and homosexuality.

2. Uncleanness or impurity *(akatharsia)* is the opposite of clean and pure. The papyri uses the word for material dirt. Hippocrates used it to describe impurities which gather around a sore or a wound. Morally, it means a mind defiled by evil thoughts and associations, that which is repulsive, disgusting and separates from God.

3. Laciviousness or indecency means throwing off all restraint, becoming wild, wanton and undisciplined; a complete disregard for public opinion and the rights of others. It describes one so reckless that he ceases to care what God or man thinks of his actions.

B. Unlawful dealings with spiritual things—misdirected faith

1. Idolatry refers to worshiping the creature rather than the Creator. In former fallen civilizations sexuality was actually worshiped. It refers to any extravagant admiration of the heart.

2. Witchcraft or sorcery *(pharmakeia)* alludes to the misuse of drugs, astrology, enchantments, etc.

C. Violations of the Golden Rule or of brotherly love

1. Hatred is the opposite of love and is that which can exist between classes of society, races and men. It is an attitude of the mind in which a person detests, abhors and despises other people.

2. Variance is the outcome or result of hatred. Though a characteristic of the pagan world, it is used four out of six times in connection with the church, as was evident at Corinth. Quarreling, wrangling and fighting are always an enemy of fellowship and unity.

3. Emulations refer to both jealousy and envy (Gal. 5:20). Jealousy is a man's sorrow that the other person possesses something that he does not. Envy is jealousy which becomes embittered to the point of desiring to prevent the other person from possessing it. It suggests hostile deeds or words in order to dispossess the other person.

4. Wrath covers "outbursts of anger," or an explosive temper which flares up suddenly and then dies as quickly. Its source is usually pride, selfishness or undue sensitivity.

5. Strife refers to selfish ambition which causes one to canvass for office by means of hired partisans. It is ambition which has no conception of service, only desire for profit and power (Phil. 1:15, 2:3; James 3:16).

6. Seditions and divisions literally mean "to stand apart from." It is where men are divided and unity is destroyed. Grounds for such may be personal, partisan, class, racial, theological or ecclesiastical (Rom. 16:17, 18; 1 Cor. 3:3-7).

7. Heresies refer to all deviations from the truth, to those who belong to organized schools of thought, such as the Pharisees and Sadducees. It includes groups and cliques who exclude from their circle all but their number. It is not necessarily erroneous doctrine, but factions which lead or fall into error.

8. Murder means to kill (in the New Testament context it is equated with hatred) (1 John 3:15).

D. Sins of excess or intemperate desires

1. Drunkenness is strongly condemned by conservative Christianity (Prov. 20:1; 23:29, 30).

2. Reveling, rioting and carousing are offensive to God and man and is a consequence of drunkenness.[1]

The contrast is further seen in the plurality of works versus the unity of the fruit. The plurality of works sug-

---

1 C. Thomas Rhyne, "The Flesh or the Spirit," *Grammatical Exegesis of Galatians*, (Cleveland, Tennessee; Lee College, December 9, 1965), pp. 5-10.

gests that which is confused, conflicting and competitive. It depicts the chaos of one lust contending against another for mastery. The singular use of "fruit" *(karpos)* means that all elements of Christian character are a unity. It is not possible to pick out one. It is either all or nothing. Such is the product of one influence—the Spirit—reproducing the believer into that one perfect pattern as seen in Jesus Christ. The Christian life is a completely harmonized and unified life with Christ at the center. One part does not take from the other, but contributes to the beauty of the whole. It is the new nature producing the Christlike fruit of the Spirit (Matt. 7:17, 12:33; Rom. 8:6). The flesh is man at work, the Spirit is God at work (Isa. 31:3).

"The Cluster"

Love heads the list. It is the foundation of the fruit of the Spirit. G. Campbell Morgan says this verse should read, "The fruit of the Spirit is love." Then the other words should simply elaborate on this word "love." The use of the collective noun "fruit" with the singular verb "is," followed by a list of nine characteristics, seems grammatically inaccurate unless we recognize the place of "love" in the whole scheme of God. Love occupies first place in the fruit, in the exercise of the gifts and in the great commandments (Matt. 22:37-39). One of the grandest statements in' the Bible is "God is love" (1 John 4:7, 8). When love is dominant we will have all the others. The life of love is a life of joy, peace, longsuffering, etc. A loveless life is a joyless and a peaceless life. Dr. Charles W. Conn says,

> It is no accident that the Bible places prime emphasis on love. In listing the fruit of the Spirit, Paul gave first place to love (Gal. 5:22). It was with good reason that

John said, "He who loves not knows not God" (1 John 4:7, 8). The Scriptures are neither mild nor scant in their declaration of love's necessity. Love must dominate our lives if we are God's children.[2]

The English language has one word for love, while the Greek language has four. *Eros* was the god of love in Greek mythology and the equivalent of the Roman god, Cupid. Eros was used for physical love or sexual desire, thus the English derivative "erotic." This word does not appear in the New Testament. Forms of the word appear in the Septuagint but generally in a dishonorable sense. Its absence is significant, as though the truth of God abstained from the defiling contact.[3] *Storge* was used to denote family affection. Plato, thus, wrote concerning parental love. It also describes love for a ruler or a nation. A kindred adjective occurs in the New Testament as *philostorgos,* which combines two Greek words for love and is translated "kindly affectioned" (Rom. 12:10). It implies that the Christian community is not a society but a family.[4] A third and most commonly used Greek word for love is *philia.* It is used of family affection, but refers primarily to friendship. It is the basis of our English derivative *filial* and is used to describe this beautiful relationship in the Scriptures (Matt. 10:37; John 11:3, 36; 20:2).

The most common New Testament word for love is *agape.* It is not a classical word at all. Trench calls it a word born within the bosom of revealed religion. . . . there is no trace of it in any heathen writer whatever.[5]

---

2 Charles W. Conn, "Love is Positive," *Church of God Evangel,* August 4, 1958, p. 3.
3 R. C. Trench, *Synonyms of the New Testament,* Wm. B. Eerdmans Pub. Co., Grand Rapids, 1963, p. 43.
4 Barclay, *op. cit.,* p. 12.
5 Trench, *op. cit.*

Vine calls it the characteristic word of Christianity, used by the Spirit of revelation to express ideas previously unknown.[6] Anders Nygren insists on the original absence of any relation between Platonic *Eros* and New Testament *Agape*. He quotes Wilamowitz-Moellendorff's great work on Plato to the effect that "Paul knew nothing of *Eros* and Plato knew nothing of *Agape*."[7]

The basic meaning of love is "action." Vine says,

> Love can be known only from the action it prompts. God's love is seen in the gift of His Son (1 John 4:9, 10).[8]

Dr. Conn says,

> Love cannot rest unexpressed; love cannot lie dormant and watch a neighbor or brother suffer need. Love cannot remain silent and hear a person slandered and maligned. Love is sensitive to the needs of others; love grasps each opportunity to help others. Love is dynamic in the human breast and compels action for the benefit of those who are loved. Love moves; it does things, it must manifest and declare itself. Where there is no action and where there is no positiveness, there is no love. You cannot say that you love a person simply because you do not desire his downfall, failure or injury. Strangers who have no pretense of love can say that much. . . . When you love, you act! You exert every energy within you, to assist, to uphold, to encourage or to save. That is why Jesus called love "the first and great commandment" (Matt. 22:37-39).[9]

Barclay says,

> *Agape* demands the exercise of the whole man. Chris-

---

6 Vine, *op. cit.,* p. 20.
7 From *Agape and Eros* by Anders Nygren, translated by Philip S. Watson. Published in the U.S.A. by The Westminster Press, Philadelphia, 1953, p. 31. Used by permission.
8 Vine, *op. cit.,* p. 21.
9 Conn, *op. cit.*

tian love must not only extend to those who love us, but to the Christian fellowship, to the neighbor, to the enemy and to all the world.[10]

Nygren summarizes the content of the Christian idea of love in four points:

1. *Agape* is spontaneous and unmotivated. When it is said that God loves man, this is not a judgment on what man is like, but on what God is like. According to Christianity, "motivated" love is human; spontaneous and "unmotivated" love is Divine. Just by the fact that it seeks sinners, who do not deserve it and can lay no claim to it, it manifests most clearly its spontaneous and unmotivated nature.

2. *Agape* is indifferent to value. Any thought of value on the part of the object is out. When God loves the sinner, it cannot be because of his sin, but in spite of his sin (Matt. 5:45).

3. *Agape* is creative. That which has no worth acquires worth just by becoming the object of God's love. *Agape* does not recognize value, but creates it. The man who is loved by God has no value in himself; what gives him value is precisely the fact that God loves him.

4. *Agape* is the initiator of fellowship with God. This means that God takes the initiative. All other ways by which man seeks to establish fellowship are futile. From man's side there is no way. God must Himself come to meet man and offer him His fellowship. *Agape* is God's way to man.[11]

It is not the nature of man to love God. It is his nature to hate—to crucify. Man is egocentric and seeks his own satisfaction and self-enhancement. It is the work of the Holy Spirit to change that fact, to minister Christ to him and transform him into the likeness of

---

10 Barclay, *op. cit.*, p. 14.
11 Nygren, *op. cit.*, pp. 75-81. Adapted.

God's dear Son. When man, through faith in the Word, is laid open to the action of God (Heb. 4:12), this *Agape* is shed abroad in his heart by the Holy Spirit (Rom. 5:5). He is no longer the same, he is a new creature in Christ. The subject is no longer man, but Christ. The life of God has taken possession of his innermost being. He lives in Christ and Christ lives and works in him (Gal. 2:20). He is constrained by the *Agape* of Christ (2 Cor. 5:14). He is led by the Spirit (Gal. 5:18), walks after the Spirit (Rom. 8:4), and bears the fruit of the Spirit (Gal. 5:22).

When God's love is shed abroad in man's heart, his life gains a new center. The emphasis is transferred from self to Christ. "I live," said Paul, "yet not I, but Christ liveth in me (Gal. 2:20)." The Christian no longer lives unto himself, but unto Him, who for his sake died and rose again (2 Cor. 5:15; Phil. 2:21). The egocentric is now Christocentric. Bondage to the ego is crucified and man stands new toward God and his neighbor (Rom. 15:1-3; Gal. 6:14). Hatred, bitterness and reaction to injury has been purged by the Spirit's fire. That "pneumatic fluid" infused by the Spirit now flows forth spontaneously. It is that outgoing, overflowing artesian spring which cannot be stopped, dammed up or fail as long as it is connected to the divine source. As long as man is open to God, love will flow through him as a channel to the brethren, to his neighbors, his enemies and the world. It will flow regardless of its receptivity or treatment. Christian love is an extension of God's love. How do I love God? I love Him by loving my neighbor and my enemy (Luke 6:27-36; 1 John 4:20, 21). The adequacy of a vertical relationship with God is relative to a horizontal relationship with our fellowmen, and we are by nature incapable of a horizontal without first a vertical. The cross means that God has reached down to us that we might reach out to others. This is actualized only as the minus sign crosses out the (ego) capital *I* (John 3:30).

No church has the right to call itself by the name of "Christ" or "God" where there is bitterness and strife. Love is the hallmark of the Christian. One of the severest handicaps of the modern church is that it often appears to the outsider to be a company of people squabbling bitterly about nothing. Men may differ and still love each other. More people have been brought into the Church by real Christian love than by all the theological arguments in the world; and more have been driven from the Church by hardness and ugliness than by all the temptations in the world.

Love is the outer manifestation of the hidden life "in Christ." C. S. Lewis says,

> Our model is the Jesus, not of Calvary, but of the workshop, the roads, the crowds, the clamorous demands and surly oppositions, the lack of all peace and privacy, the interruptions. For this is divine life operating under human conditions.[12]

Clarence Jordan paraphrases,

> Love has no false face. Shun evil and hang on to good. I mean: in brotherliness, show genuine concern for one another; in courtesy, putting others above yourselves; in enthusiasm, never letting up; in morale, glowing; in the Lord's work, slaving; in hope, bubbling over; in trouble, taking it; in prayer, keeping it up; in meeting the needs of church members, sharing; in hospitality, going out of your way. Bless those who

---

12 C. S. Lewis, *The Four Loves*, Harcourt, Brace and World Inc., New York, 1960, p. 17.

do you in. Bless them, I say, and don't cuss them. Join in the fun with those having fun; join in the tears with those shedding tears. Treat each other equally; pay no special attention to the upper crust, but mingle freely with the lower class people. And don't scratch each other's back. Never return evil for evil. Have respect for things which everybody else considers worthwhile. If it's possible—that is, from your side— Wage Peace With All Mankind. Don't take vengence into your own hands, my dear ones, but rather make room for another's wrath. For the Bible says, "Revenge is my job," says the Lord, "I will tend to it." But if your enemy hungers, bread him, if he thirsts, water him. In this way you'll fill his noggin with lighted charcoal. Don't be overwhelmed by evil, but overwhelm evil with good (Rom. 12:9-21).[13]

This is what love is like and this is the way love acts in life situations. If we are Christ's, then we ought to live a life suitable with that fact.

If love is the foundation of the cluster, then joy is the superstructure. The New Testament is a book of joy and Christ is the source of joy. The believer's joy begins with his acceptance of Jesus as Saviour and it continues to be the atmosphere of his Christian life. Joy is another distinguishing grace of the Christian Church. It is an expression of delight in God because of salvation in Christ. It is a cheerful gladness which characterizes the demeanor of every believer and his relations with others. It is not that which comes from the absence of trouble, the presence of desirable circumstances, or mental conditioning. It is the product of the Spirit and not human effort or adjustment. It exists where temporal joys cannot survive. It is a manifestation of the Holy Spirit and therefore beyond natural explanation.

---

13 Jordon, *op. cit.*, pp. 38, 39.

M. G. McLuhan's treatise on "Joy" is most enlightening.

> As the child of God develops, his joy becomes deeper and more mature. The progressive sequence can be explained in the following ways: (a) The joy of initial spiritual experiences. God does not expect the Christian to spend the rest of his earthly life reveling in the joys of spiritual experience. Many Christians never progress beyond this point. Their entire concept of the Christian religion is totally introvertive and selfish. It is an endless sequence of "getting blessed" or "receiving blessings." God expects us to graduate to a more gratifying joy. (b) The joy of spiritual development. The child of God moves out of the sanctuary of initial experiences into the challenge of living victoriously over the world, of experiencing joy in hardship, persecution and affliction with stabilizing delight. (c) The joy of Christian service. He must not succumb to apathy or self-glory; but must move out into the world of sinners by obeying the great commission. His joy of being and achieving must be enhanced by producing. He cannot camp in the sanctuary, but must get out and experience the joy of witnessing, winning souls and showing forth compassion for others. Many selfish "blessing-minded" Christians never experience the rare joy of serving others. (d) The unwavering joy of the Lord. This is the highest and final phase. There will come times when experiences seem cold and work unrewarding. At this point many have fallen by the wayside because they knew nothing of the joy which rests upon the unchangeable promises of God. The joy of the Lord is the true strength of God's people (Neh. 8:10).[14]

Peace is the crown of the cluster. It is the English translation of the Hebrew greeting "shalom." To the Hebrews it meant "well being," to the Latins—a reciprocal legal relationship, to the Greeks—an interlude in an ever-

---

14 M. G. McLuhan, "The Fruit of the Spirit," pp. 1-3.

lasting war. In Rabbinical literature it meant the portion of the righteous, in the Septuagint—the prosperity and good which only God can bring. To the earlier historians it meant concord between men, but in our time it is synonymous with the ends of a particular ideology. Basically and originally "peace" is a religious term.

In the New Testament the principle meaning of peace *(eirene)* is "salvation"—the salvation of the whole man —complete reconciliation with God. In its widest sense it is the normal, healthy state which corresponds to the will of God. It is that Christian temperament and religious disposition which is freed from tension and guilt. As a gift, it is either to be received or rejected. Christ makes peace and is peace. It is that by which unity is maintained (Eph. 4:3). Peace is the wholesome condition of the church in the face of strife, disputes and factions (2 Tim. 2:22, 23). It is the seed from which righteousness grows as a fruit (Heb. 12:11; James 3:17, 18).

Peace is the tranquil state of the soul assured of salvation (Matt. 5:9; Rom. 5:1). It is a reconciliation not only with God, but between man and his neighbor. It is a completely new dimension which fosters right relationships in every sphere of life—at home, at church and on the job. Peace for the Christian is not the absence of tribulation—Jesus and Paul are examples of this. Peace is not the absence of conflict and trouble, but is the presence of God in the midst of them. Paul put it like this, "Let the peace of God rule in your hearts" (Col. 3:15)—*rule,* meaning "to preside, arbitrate and umpire." Again Paul turns man's heart into a castle when he calls peace to garrison and guard the soul of man against its enemies (Phil. 4:7).

Politicians are concerned about outward peace. Christians, however, are concerned with real peace which is both inward and outward. Billy Graham says, "If by peace we mean appeasing tyranny, compromising with gangsters and being silent because we haven't the moral fortitude to speak out against injustice, then this is not real peace. It is a false peace, a farce and a hoax."[15] Real peace can only come from God, for it is impossible to love God and hate your brother. Jesus emphasized our peacemaking and peace-keeping role when He pointed toward our brother, our neighbor and beyond, to our enemy. What a day for bearing the fruit of peace! When the highest genius is devoted to destruction, the biggest business is the sponsorship of war and the loudest voices are those crying out in hate, what a time for men of God to bear the Christlike fruit of "peace on earth, good will toward men!" What a time for God to speak peace through His people, the peace that passeth all understanding and misunderstanding!

Paul now illustrates the Golden Rule which the Holy Spirit produces in the believer by longsuffering, gentleness and goodness. Longsuffering (makrothumia) is a compound of makros meaning "long" and thumos meaning "temper." It is the opposite of thumoi or "anger" (Gal. 5:20), and refers to that long-spirited, patient endurance under injuries inflicted by others. It means "to bear with it"—that quality of self-restraint in the face of provocation. God's mercy toward the world and His tender attitude toward man illustrates the point (Psa. 103:8). Should the strict justice of God prevail, all mankind would be swept into judgment. While the modern

---

15 Cort R. Flint, *The Quotable Billy Graham*, (Anderson, South Carolina; Drake House Publishers, 1966), p. 146.

world has gone mad over speed, it is comforting to know that some slowness still exists. Perseverance in bearing trouble and slowness in avenging wrongs are needed in our time (Rom. 2:4; 2 Peter 3:9). Man is not qualified to administer vengeance (Rom. 12:19).

Longsuffering is manifested basically to people and patience is manifested toward things. Longsuffering has the power to avenge, yet refrains. Patience (*hupomene*) has no choice except to be patient. The Christian chooses the former. Longsuffering is a long holding out of the mind before it gives room to action or passion (Eph. 4:2). Perseverance is that brave patience by which the Christian contends against the hindrances, persecutions and temptations of the inside and outside world (1 Thess. 1:3; 2 Tim. 2:4). Longsuffering is long-tempered, the opposite of short-tempered. It does not mean being long-faced, but is the power to bear irritating events and irritating people without being irritated.

Gentleness is often translated kindness. It refers to a kindly disposition toward one's fellowman, treating others the way God has treated us (Eph. 4:31, 32). Like love it is an activity rather than an attitude. Gentleness (*crestotes*) is goodness that shows itself in benevolence and kindness (Mark 9:41). It means being fit for use —beneficient—a useful and useable person. We often interpret its meaning to the contrary as being too soft for use. Gentleness is a beautiful word which expresses a grace that is not identical to goodness. Goodness is that sterling quality which is apart from attractiveness, where-as, gentleness is the attractiveness of goodness. Donald Gee aptly states:

> We must be careful to understand that gentleness is never the result of weakness. It requires great strength

> to be truly gentle. Weak characters are often rough
> and unkind just because they are weak. They despise
> the quality of the "gentleness of Christ," and think it
> manifests lack of strength. The opposite is true. Gen-
> tleness is strength under perfect control. . . . New
> converts deserve gentle and sympathetic treatment from
> older Christians. Matters of "separation" are sometimes
> roughly treated, where gentleness would win an easy
> response. . . . Truly "strong" Christians can be gentle
> just because they are strong (Rom. 15:1).[16]

Far from being a mere grace of word and countenance, gentleness pervades and penetrates the whole nature. It mellows that which would have been harsh and austere and eases that which would have been rough and galling (Matt. 11:30; Luke 7:39). Gentleness was the pre-dominating characteristic of Christ's ministry in His gracious dealings with man (Luke 7:37-50).

"Goodness" is a biblical word not found in secular Greek. It is the New Testament translation of *agathosune* and occurs nowhere else except in the Greek translation of the Old Testament. Trench calls it one of many words which revealed religion has given to later language. It is a word of energy and activity whose zeal may be seen rebuking, correcting and chastising (Matt. 21:13; chap. 23). Vine suggests it to be that goodness of character and constitution which is morally honorable, pleasing to God and therefore beneficial. Goodness is that which Christians are to prove (Rom. 12:2), cleave to (12:9), do (13:3), work at (2:10), follow after (1 Thess. 5: 15), be zealous of (1 Peter 3:13), imitate (3 John 2) and overcome evil with (Rom. 12:21).

God is essentially, absolutely and consumately good

---

16 Donald Gee, *Fruitful or Barren*, (Springfield, Missouri, Gospel Pub-lishing House, 1961) pp. 25-29. Used by permission.

(Matt. 19:17; Mark 10:18; Luke 18:19). When tracing the fruit down to its roots, its source is found in God. Are we not exhorted to praise the Lord for His goodness (Psa. 107:31)? Did not Jesus assert, "There is none good but one, that is God" (Matt. 19:17)? It is God's goodness that leads us to repentance (Rom. 2:4). Yet, in the face of problems and pain, man is tempted to doubt the goodness of God. How hard it is for man to reconcile the objective providence of God with his subjective ideas of what ought to be. God is good, He is the Fountain of all goodness and we who are filled with His Spirit will manifest that goodness.

M. G. McLuhan says,

> Goodness applies to character as an inner quality. It is the goodness of God manifested through His children. It carries with it moral and spiritual "saltiness" that may not always please others, but has their best interest at heart.[17]

This does not refer to that goody-goody suffocating sweetness which smothers everyone with a mushy sentimentality. Such phoney gushiness is a cover-up, either for guilt or insecurity. Goodness is often distorted and made unattractive by those who labor so painfully and obviously at being good. Like the Pharisees, they are obsessed with things and doing rather than being. They make themselves and everybody around them miserable. This is what the little girl meant when she prayed, "Dear Jesus, make all the bad people good, and all the good people nice." Jesus ridiculed this kind of goodness and called those that practiced it hypocrites—straining at gnats while swallowing camels.

---

17 M. G. McLuhan, "The Holy Spirit's Work in Regeneration and Sanctification," *op. cit.*, p. 4.

Barnabas was "a good man, and full of the Holy Ghost and of faith" (Acts 11:24). God's people must be upright and honest as well as capable. Ability must be harnessed by that which is noble and pure. Cleverness will carry a man for a while, but will fail miserably unless it is matched by stability. Sad to say, but it is possible for one to do good without being good. A murderer can be generous. A prostitute can be kind. A liar can be thoughtful. A thief can be a Robinhood, robbing the rich to help the poor. Even Thomas Paine, the infidel, could say, "My religion is to do good." Far more important than doing good is being good. To be good is not a do-it-yourself job. It takes outside help that can only come from God.

Christ is our ideal standard and pattern of goodness. When we accept Him as the Lord of our life, the Spirit begins to alter our thoughts, attitudes and actions after His pattern of goodness. Any goodness which we exhibit is an outward expression of an inner reality. The reward is not in what we get, but in what we become. It is not in "making good" or "doing good," but in "being good." How thankful we should be for good leaders, a good heritage and for men—produced by the Spirit—who have led us into the goodness of God. Whatever else we have, let us have good men who are examples of Christlikeness. Whatever else a preacher is, let him first be a good man. This is true for teachers, officials, leaders, officers and for all who claim to be Christian.

Faith is best understood as "faithfulness," meaning one who is "full of faith." Vine translates it "trustworthiness," Phillips and Moffatt "fidelity" and Jordan "loyalty." This seventh grace is the only one listed as one of the gifts and also the fruit (1 Cor. 12:9; Gal. 5:22).

Faith the gift is power for doing. Faith the grace is character for being. Faith, meekness and temperance all refer to conduct. The fruit of faith is trustworthiness and honesty in one's treatment of others. It means the ethical virtue of reliability. If I have a choice, give me the "faithful" man, for ability is only a part of dependability. It is trustworthiness in human relations begotten of our assurance of God's faithfulness to us. Such is not manifested in an "up and down" experience, or a sporadic kind of service, but rather is as constant and dependable as the Holy Spirit who produces it. The Bible commends the faithful (Matt. 25:23; Rev. 2:10).

Meekness is probably the most unpopular and misunderstood of all Christian virtues. As the opposite of the spirit of this world, it is not greasy servility or flabbiness. Meekness is not weakness, but power under control and power that is properly channeled. Rather than a horse running wild, it is one with harness, bridle, bit and someone holding the reins (Num. 12:3; Matt. 5:5); like lightning and electricity, the difference being that of control. Meekness is a balance between strength and gentleness, or as Aristotle called it, "the middle quality between fierceness and spinelessness." It is the explosive might of the passions, harnessed by the Spirit in the service of God and man.

Meekness is exercised first and chiefly toward God (Matt. 11:29; James 1:21). How we need an unquestioning acceptance of God's dealings as being wise and good without disputing, resisting or even understanding. Only the humble heart is meek, and as such, does not fight, struggle or contend against God. Pride and arrogance are the passions difficult to guide, whereas, "tolerance" (J. B. Phillips translation of meekness), can be readily directed in the will of God. Meekness is our surrender to "whatever" the will of God holds for us. The natural man pushes to get what he wants, yet in the getting it turns to ashes. The meek only want to inherit what the Father has willed. Restlessness and panic often reign where this grace has not been cultivated or allowed to grow. Meekness is heaven's tranquilizer. It is that quiet acceptance of a greater will than our own that brings us into harmony with things as God plans them. The meek shall "inherit the earth," because the meek are those who are governed by the Spirit.

Temperance is the conclusion of the cluster and refers to "self-control." The word *enkrateia* is from *kratos* meaning "strength." It signifies mastery, dominion and power over one's self, such as self-command, self-restraint or the opposite of self-indulgence. Literally it means "to grasp" or "to hold in." It covers every form of self-control including the appetites, tempers, passions, lusts, and inordinate desires. Temperance suggests mastery over all desires. It is the grace by which the flesh is controlled. Samson is an example of great power, but a lack of control where natural appetites were concerned. His outward strength was not matched by inward strength. It was when Paul reasoned of temperance that Felix trembled, for he had failed to control his passions (Acts 24:25). Any intemperate leader will damage the local testimony (Titus 2:2).

Temperance must clothe the total man. He must be physically disciplined, neither engaging in self-abuse by overindulgence or by over-denial. The Christian life is not all feasting or all fasting. It is a balanced, wholesome and healthy life. Let us be on guard toward the fleshly lusts that war against the soul, for lack of control here will produce disastrous results (1 Peter 2:11). The disciplined Christian wins the prize.

We must be emotionally temperate. Our extrovertive behaviour must be that of stability and balance, lest by catering to extremes we become temperamental. Many go overboard on the sheer enjoyment of religion, while others try to ration the abundance of God. Sweetness always tempts toward excess (Prov. 25:16). Even the tongue needs to "hold itself in" lest it offend one of these little ones (1 Tim. 2:8; Titus 2:6, 7; James 1:26, 3:2).

Temperance of the mentality will bring body, soul and spirit to task. This refers to our introvertive deportment. The spirit of man is capable of strong feelings. Such, is not to recommend repression, but rather consecration—a surrender of one's total self to God, so that the Holy Spirit has complete control. There need be no conflict between Pentecostal inspiration and Pentecostal self-control, for the gifts of power and the fruit of conduct are from the same source. When the Holy Spirit is at the controls, all areas of life will be brought under the Lordship of Jesus Christ. Power is then all the greater and the effect more lasting when used with a holy temperance. Intemperance is often the chief reason for the lack of power.

"The Cultivation"

Fruit indicates a harvest. The yield of the harvest and the maturity of the fruit is related to the cultivation. A favorite picture of the process is painted by Christ in the Gospel of St. John (John 15). Three things are important, (1) abiding, (2) purging and (3) yielding.

Abiding is that essential factor in fruit-bearing. Fruitage in the Spirit requires rootage in the Spirit. Life is necessary to fruit-bearing and comes singularly through Christ, the True Vine. Without this vital connection it is impossible to bear fruit. Apart from Him, the disciple can do nothing (John 15:4, 5). It is the work of the Spirit to keep the branches in vital contact with the Vine. Then the life (sap) will flow and love, like blood through the body, will bring health and a holy yield unto God. The test of abiding is obedience to His commandments and a following of His example (John 15:10; 1 John 2:5, 6, 24; 3:6, 24; 4:12, 13, 16). To abide is to obey.

Abiding is the positive side and purging is the negative. The cultivation is not ours, but the Father's. He is the husbandman—the Lord of the vineyard. The care of the vineyard includes taking away, purging (pruning), cleaning and culling (choosing). (See John 15:2, 3, 16). Dead posts produce no fruit, neither can fruit come from dead and unhealthy trees. When Jesus found no figs on the tree, He demanded that it be cut down (Luke 13:6-9). The branch that bears no fruit, "He taketh away." There is an antagonism between the Christian life of fruitfulness and the sinful death of barrenness. It is impossible for the unregenerate to manifest the fruit of the Spirit. The productive person is a redeemed person. It is not by generation, but by regeneration. These marks distinguish the godly from the ungodly (Matt. 7:16).

The yield is the result of the abiding and the purging. The classification of yield is (a) no fruit, (b) fruit, (c) more fruit and (d) much fruit. Two things are apparent: (1) the indispensable expectation of yield from the vineyard by the Husbandman; and (2) the action of His skills applied toward increased and peak production. You and I are not surprised to find apples on an apple tree or clusters hanging from a vine. Jesus was disturbed, however, when He saw a tree with leaves but no fruit. He promptly pronounced its demise (Matt. 21: 18-20). "Every branch," He said, indicating that all Christians are to bear fruit. Fruit-bearing is not a description of the exceptional Christian, but of every Christian. All are meant to manifest fruit. The harvest of the Spirit is not a natural result like something growing wild. It is fruit that is cultivated and produced by the Spirit Himself. The Spirit produces His own fruit as we trust and cooperate. We do not live like this and hope to become Christians, but we live like this because we are Christians. Christlikeness and fruitfulness are one and the same. The fruit of the Spirit and the Christ-life are synonymous. Paul's picture of the nine graces of the Spirit has been acclaimed as his "Portrait of Christ." Paul's painting was intended, however, to be a portrait of those who are Christ's—who bear His name, His reproach and His fruit (John 15:8; Phil. 4:17).

5

The Holy Spirit and the Contemporary Scene

"Many shall come in my name" (Matt. 24:5).
"Try the spirits whether they are of God" (1 John 4:1).

God the Holy Spirit has always been involved in man's existence. Directly and indirectly He executes the design of God on this earth. The basic instrument through which He works is man. The agency with which He works is the church and the guidebook by which He works is the Bible. This chapter will concern the scene of the secular and the sacred in the light of the Scriptures. It will deal primarily with traditionalism, Ecumenism, Evangelicalism, Pentecostalism and neo-Pentecostalism.

The *secular* scene is one of change and revolution As Heraclitus describes it, "Everything is in a state of change except the law of change." Our lives are constantly being swept by the winds of change. No sooner

than we get accustomed to a new thing, it is replaced by
something newer. Revolution is the order of the day.
The only way to have something new, they say, is to
tear down the old, and so the cycle begins. Our society
is incapable of shock and our generation is agog on ex-
perimentation. The prevalent eroticism in arts, the sexual
permissiveness, the drug culture, the rise in crime and
other violence all point to the erosion of morality and
authority. Obscenity, the risque, the vulgar and the suggestive are having a heyday and it is not getting better.
Man has ruled God out and allowed everything else in.
Our society could be the successor to Babel and Rome.

Speaking before the twenty-sixth annual conference of
the Pentecostal Fellowship of North America, Dr. R.
Leonard Carroll said, "This day is pregnant with destiny.
It is not, however, a new phenomenon. Such explosive-
ness, uncontrollability and unpleasantness have always
been at the end of the sinful spectrum. Sin always de-
ludes and damns."[1] Dr. Carl F. H. Henry writes, "Our
century of crises now faces a final choice between world
evangelism or world revolution. The near future is between Christ and Antichrist. Swaying in the balance is
the fate of all mankind."[2]

The *sacred* scene is as changing and revolutionary as
the secular. Some have asked, "Is the church converting
the world or is the world converting the church?" Christianity is needlessly losing ground. Fewer than one third
of the world's inhabitants are now identified with Christendom, and Christians are being outpaced by population growth and revivals in other religions. The Christian

---

1 R. Leonard Carroll, "Pentecostal Bonds in a Fragmented Society,"
Church of God Evangel (Pathway Press, December 1, 1969), p. 4.
2 Carl F. H. Henry, "World Evangelism or World Revolution," *Church
of God Evangel* (July 25, 1966), p. 6.

community is a diminishing minority.[3] In its "Decade of the Sixties Summation on Religion," *Time* magazine states: "The most notable fact in religion today is that ministers of all denominations are trying, somewhat desperately, to find new ways to carry God back into the everyday life of society and to make Him, in the prevailing cliché of the day, relevant."[4] Dr. Dale Moody, a Baptist theologian teaching in Rome's Pontifical Gregorian University believes, "God is giving the church a good shaking. With His left hand He disturbs her slumber with the noise of social revolution, and with His right hand He rings the bell calling for relevance to such pressing problems as race, poverty and war. A polarity develops in every denomination of Christianity between those calling for old-fashioned soulwinning and those new styles of social action that shock and startle the faithful."[5]

Carl F. H. Henry blames the theologians for much of the modern malaise.

> Today many theologians need to be evangelized. They are prime examples of religious confusion, zestfully contradicting each other in the name of progress. Some ardently promote secular rather than supernatural perspectives and eagerly undermine the faith of the Bible. These deviant radicals draw salaries from Christian institutions founded for the promulgation of Christ's gospel, and piously plead missionary concern as an excuse for their defection from the faith. They stick the label of mythology on the miracles and try to seal the living God in a casket. Professedly to make Christianity relevant . . . they administer the "last rites" to

---

3 Stan Mooneyham, "One Race, One Gospel, One Task," *Church of God Evangel* (May 16, 1966), p. 19.

4 "The New Ministry: Bringing God Back to Life," *Time* (December 26, 1969), p. 40. Reprinted by permission from *Time*, The Weekly Newsmagazine; Copyright Time Inc. 1969.

5 *Ibid.*, p. 40.

> evangelical Christianity and leave modern man still in
> desperate need of spiritual help and salvation. These
> newfangled notions have so revised New Testament
> evangelism that the devil himself must be tempted to
> become the very first convert.[6]

The demand for change has taken its toll among the traditional movements of religion. The Catholic Church has been most affected in this sense. Such traditionally untouchables as their liturgy, hymnody, latin mass, celibacy, papal infallibility, birth control encyclicals and the garb of its convent women are now being changed or reevaluated. "Protestant seminary enrollments are slightly up, but Catholic enrollments are dropping drastically. As many as 4,000 U.S. priests leave the priesthood each year. Often they include some of the ablest men. Something has prompted such men to abandon the old forms. For some it is frustration with a system of authority that seems overbearing and out of date."[7]

The predictions for the coming decade include optional celibacy, an increasingly democratic church with laymen choosing their ministers and the lines between priest and laymen fading. Its women may be ordained and its laymen may celebrate the Eucharist.[8]

The criterion for Traditionalism is that tradition must be measured by truth. Truth is that which God has to say about the matter (Rom. 3:4). Traditions that are based on truth are to remain and to be carried out (1 Cor. 11:2; 2 Thess. 2:15, 3:6). Traditions that are not founded upon the Scriptures are judged as the traditions of men which are often used in competition with and in opposition to the commandments of God (Matt. 15:

---

6 Henry, *op. cit.,* pp. 6, 7.
7 *Time,* p. 40.
8 *Ibid.,* p. 45.

2-6; Mark 7:3-13; Gal. 1:14; Col. 2:8; 1 Peter 1:18). Tradition for tradition's sake is not reason enough. Only as it meets the criterion of truth as found in the Scriptures is it worthy of a hearing. The charge of irrelevance has been true in many instances because of the historic bondage to tradition. Truth, however, is eternally contemporary. It is not based on tradition, but upon the revelation of God in Jesus Christ as revealed in the Spirit-inspired Scriptures (2 Peter 1:21).

Another part of the sacred scene is Ecumenism. The term "ecumenical" comes from the Greek word *oikoumene,* meaning "this inhabited world." It is used to represent God's children from every part of the earth. The goal of Ecumenism is the establishment of one great world church. Its plan calls first for the merging of all Protestant bodies into one; second, the uniting of Protestants and Catholics and finally, the bringing of all religions including Buddhism, Hinduism and the Moslems under one roof. The strategy calls for the creation of a National Church in every land, thus the present National Council of Churches (N.C.C.). National Councils are a part of the World Council of Churches (W.C.C.), all of which are working toward a world power or a superchurch. The idea is said to be one of unity. To attain this there must be a denial of the basic doctrines of distinctives as much as possible.[9]

Dr. John A. Mackay questions the goals of Ecumenicalism.

> . . . Dynamic missionary effort gave birth to the "ecumenical" and also the movement toward unity . . . But now unity is not for mission. Unity is for unity . . .

9 Richard W. DeHaan, "The Coming World Church," Radio Bible Class, Grand Rapids, Mich., March, 1969, pp. 3, 4.

> Should not priority be given to a united movement
> toward spiritual awakening rather than a top-level, ec-
> clesiastical effort to merge church denominations in a
> single organizational structure? Might it not happen
> that the Christian Future may lie with a reformed
> Catholicism and a matured Pentecostalism?[10]

Dr. Walter C. Hobbs says,

> Over the years tradition has sanctified the church and
> men have turned it in their thinking from a means
> into an end. The organized church is to be perceived
> and used as an instrument, not an idol.[11]

H. K. Stothard comments:

> To accept the notion that the world's religions are all
> useful ways of achieving universal salvation is to make
> a mockery of the core of the New Testament message.
> A genuinely biblical understanding of the Incarnation
> and the Atonement rejects once and for all every sug-
> gestion of inclusiveness. Writes G. W. Bromiley, "The
> fact that Christian life begins with the sovereign act
> of the Spirit, destroys comparative religion at the root
> and rules out the Pelagian heresy of self-salvation."
> The vital and indispensable role of the Holy Spirit in
> the Christian religion makes Christianity to stand dis-
> tinct, exclusive and supreme as the only true religion.[12]

In the Old Testament there were those who thought
that the Ark of God was falling and therefore should
have the steadying hand of man (2 Sam. 6:6, 7). This
was a costly conclusion. Today the "ol' ship of Zion" has

---

10 John A. Mackay, "Ecumenicalism: Threat to Christian Unity?"
Christianity Today, September 12, 1969, p. 12. Copyright 1969 *Christianity Today*; reprinted by permission.

11 Walter C. Hobbs, "The Contemporary Church: Instrument or Idol?"
Christianity Today, June 6, 1969, p. 8. Copyright 1969 *Christianity Today*;
reprinted by permission.

12 H. K. Stothard, "The One True Religion," *Christianity Today*,
August 1, 1969, p. 11. Copyright 1969 by *Christianity Today*; reprinted by
permission.

been accused of springing a leak and floundering in an uncertain sea. Those rushing to her aid seem to have neither the speed nor the skill to assist, and so they simply surmise and speculate as to the reason for her present condition.

The charge of irrelevance, though applicable in some areas, has been overplayed in others. While some are calling for relevance, others are appealing for reverence; one for inclusiveness at any price; others know that unity can only come under the wings of the Word of God. All true Christians can be united only in Jesus Christ. *Time* Magazine predicts: "Ecumenism may well be halted at the formal institutional level as various denominations grow to cherish their distinctive characteristics all over again."[13] It is interesting to note that the earliest goals of the Church of God were, first, to preserve primitive Christianity, and second, to bring about the union of all believers. We believe we have and are continuing to pursue the first and prayerfully seek the second without losing the first (John 17:11, 21-23).

Evangelicalism is founded upon the five basic principles of fundamentalism; namely, the inerrancy of the Scriptures, the Virgin Birth, the substitutionary Atonement, the physical Resurrection and the imminent physical return of the Lord Jesus Christ. A strong force in Evangelicalism is the National Association of Evangelicals. It is largely composed of the conservative side of American Protestantism. Dedicated to the relevant exposition of the Bible, Evangelicalism is for some twenty million Protestants the only alternative to neoorthodoxy and neoliberalism.

---

13 *Time, op. cit.,* p. 45.

"Where are the Evangelical Protestants in the world conflict today?" asks one of its leading theologians.

> The dominant climate is no longer protestant and is less evangelical. We are content to condemn . . . and bequeath to ecumenical forces the opportunity of elaborating Christian social ethics. The result is the evasion of the question and the evasion of social responsibility. The world has the initiative and we seem resigned forever to merely react to that initiative. We answer back with old clichés, as if there is nothing new or different. This is a transition time. It is a time of turning. The question is will we turn our backs or our hearts? We must address the trial and trouble of the needy masses. Evangelicals must begin to face the trends, search them to their depths, lay bare their weaknesses and flash the gospel's power upon them with the courage of the Apostle Paul before a Pagan Empire.[14]

Christian Life's Robert Walker says, "Twentieth century Evangelicalism is faced with a decision. It can stick to a lot of unnecessary traditional baggage in the form of customs, practices and lingo, or it can recognize that it has the opportunity to state the truths of the Christian faith in new terms and by new methods."[15]

In his "Development of the Evangelical Movement in the Twentieth Century," Cecil B. Knight identifies a new evangelicalism.

> While some Evangelicals are concerned with preserving, the New Evangelicals are busy proclaiming God's redemptive love, wisdom and power as revealed in Jesus Christ. In search for a new theology the contemporary Evangelicals are impelled to disown both the modernist perversion of biblical theology and the fundamentalist

---

14 Carl F. H. Henry, "Theological Trends Facing Evangelicals Today," NAE Convention, April 13, 1961, Grand Rapids, Michigan.

15 Robert Walker, "Is Evangelical Theology Changing?" *Christian Life,* March, 1956, p. 19.

reduction of it as well. Their hope is for a "recovery of the Apostolic perspective," and a dedication to biblical theology. Their plea is for positive triumphant preaching rather than the usual couching of basic doctrines in a negative context.[16]

One of the most outstanding contemporary evangelicals is Billy Graham. Commenting on the World Congress on Evangelism, he said,

Our prayer is that the church will receive renewed power and a sense of urgency such as was characteristic of the Early Church after Pentecost.[17]

It should be said that the Church of God is evangelical. It has been a part of NAE since its exploratory meeting April 7, 1942, and its founding in 1943. Beyond being evangelical in all points of faith and practice, the Church of God is also Pentecostal. In fact the two largest member denominations of NAE are Pentecostal—the Assemblies of God and the Church of God (Cleveland, Tennessee).[18] By being Pentecostal, the Church of God simply goes beyond the evangelical stated position, but is not contradictory to it.

Evangelical and holiness movements may be categorized by their relationship to the Pentecostal experience as follows: (1) those who believe in the work of the Holy Spirit, but do not believe in a distinctive Spirit baptism; (2) those who believe in an experience of sanctification or a second definite work of grace, but do not believe in a "third blessing" or Spirit baptism; (3) those who believe and teach a second blessing, but confuse

16 Cecil B. Knight, "The Development of the Evangelical Movement in the Twentieth Century," research paper, Butler University, 1966, pp. 35, 36.

17 Mooneyham, op. cit.

18 Hollis Green, "Pentecostals Are Evangelicals," On Guard (Dec., 1968), p. 16.

it with, or fuse it into the Holy Spirit baptism and therefore strongly deny the glossolalia phenomenon; (4) those who believe and teach the Holy Spirit baptism as an experience, but are passive in regard to sanctification or the separated life; and (5) those who believe and teach the work of the Holy Spirit in regeneration, sanctification and a definite experience of the Spirit baptism with the accompanying glossolalia phenomenon as the initial evidence. Standing in separate categories are the Latter Rain groups, the non-Trinitarians and the neo-Pentecostals, all of which may be involved in one or more of the above.

The center of Pentecostalism is the World Pentecostal Fellowship, of which the Pentecostal Fellowship of North America is an affiliate. The statement of faith for PFNA and NAE are strikingly similar with the exception of article five of the Pentecostal statement which reads, "We believe that the full gospel includes holiness of heart and life, healing for the body, and the baptism of the Holy Spirit with the initial evidence of speaking in other tongues as the Spirit gives utterance."[19]

Historically, contemporary Pentecostalism had its rebirth in revivalism. It came about at the turn of the century when revival broke out in America and many areas of the world. The holiness revivals of the late nineteenth century prepared the way for the Pentecostal revival. Originally there was no intention to start another movement. The people merely desired revival within their cold and formal churches. When reformation seemed impossible, it was either compromise or be ejected. Only then did the groups agree to organize along biblical lines.

---

19 Cecil B. Knight, "An Historical Study of Distinctions Among the Divergent Grouping of American Pentecostalism," graduate thesis, Butler University, p. 4.

A burning desire to be filled with the Spirit caused emphasis to be placed on the Holy Spirit, resulting in the authentication of an experience as received in the New Testament Church. Twentieth Century Pentecostalism, therefore, places its ultimate beginning with the First Century (Acts 1:5; 2:16, 17). The language of church history now includes the terms Pentecostals and the Pentecostal Movement. And rightly so, due to a phenomenal growth from a few hundred constituents to over two million in America,[20] and some ten to twenty million in the world.[21] Recorded alongside Catholicism and classical Protestantism, Pentecostalism has come to be known as "the third force."

Structurally, the four basic groups among the Pentecostals in America are Assemblies of God, Church of God, Pentecostal Holiness Church and the International Church of the Foursquare Gospel. Their organizational structures are congregational, both episcopal and congregational, episcopal and modified episcopal. There are numerous other organized and independent Pentecostal groups.

The governing voice of the Church of God is its General Assembly composed of both ministry and laity. In its first meeting in January, 1906, it was decided that this body was not to formulate rules and bylaws by which to govern itself, nor should it be headed by executive powers to steer and initiate its activities, but that it should judiciously govern itself by common interpretation of the

---

20 Louis Cassels, "Religion in America—Pentecostals," United Press International.

21 Ray H. Hughes, "The Latter Day Outpouring—Part II," Forward in Faith, Cleveland, Tennessee, p. 12. Robert Johnson, David L. Dungan, Hollis L. Green, "How Valuable Is Speaking in Tongues?" Church of God Evangel (August 18, 1969). p. 4.

Scriptures. The resolution passed and since reiterated states, "We do not consider ourselves a legislative or executive body, but judicial only." The original purpose of the General Assembly was for fellowship, worship and searching the Scriptures. Two of its guiding principles are: 1. The Church of God stands for the whole Bible rightly divided, and for the New Testament as the only rule for government and discipline. 2. We meet together in biennial conference to search the Scriptures and to put them into practice.

Doctrinally, Pentecostalism is orthodox and evangelical as has already been pointed out. It is also Protestant. R. H. Gause sheds light on this subject:

> The characterization of the Protestant as a protester is a bit misleading. The basic meaning of the word is "to speak forth," "to assert," "to make a witness of faith," etc. More than an "anti-movement" against something, Protestantism is a protest for original Christianity. The spirit of Protestantism is to state positively and to affirm solemnly the genuine faith of the Early Church. The doctrines which form the essence of Protestantism are: (1) Justification by faith alone, (2) the absolute authority of Scripture, and (3) the universal priesthood of believers.[22]

Evidentially, the Pentecostals are doing the job. Charles W. Conn states:

> Unless the Pentecostal Movement has a reason for existing, it has no right to exist. There are three general areas of responsibility that test this right of existence. To consider this matter frankly one must ask, "Does the Pentecostal faith honor and glorify Christ? Does the Pentecostal doctrine adhere strictly to the Word of God?

---

[22] R. H. Gause, Jr., "Pentecostal Movement in Protestant Tradition," *Church of God Evangel* (October 29, 1956), p. 4.

> Do the Pentecostal churches benefit society and the individual?"[23]

"Watch the Pentecostals," Methodist Bob Shuler urged a few years ago. "Mass evangelism is coming back and the fiery, Holy Ghost filled preachers are leading it. God is using the Pentecostals and others like them. They are making converts; they are building little churches everywhere. People are kneeling at their altars. They are the fastest growing religious movements of these tragic days."[24] While the Roman Catholic Church seethes with change and Protestantism is sitting around with a bad case of the blahs, Pentecostals are moving forward. A current communique announces, "Church of God Ahead of the Population Growth. A 237.5 percentage growth during the past twenty-four years (1945-1969) was recently reported by C. R. Spain, General Secretary-Treasurer of the Church of God, Cleveland, Tennessee. The population of the United States increased 50.9 percent during this twenty-four year period."[25] A local bulletin proclaims, "The revival goes on unabated."

> The unplanned and unannounced revival which broke more than a month ago is still with us. More than forty people have received the baptism in the Holy Spirit. For the past three Sunday nights we have had to open the chapel to accommodate the seekers in the altar. An awakening has taken place among our people and a most intensive witnessing program is resulting from the revival spirit.[26]

---

23 Conn, *Pillars of Pentecost, op. cit.,* p. 17.

24 Lewis J. Willis, "Watch the Pentecostals," *Church of God Evangel* (Nov. 13, 1967), p. 3.

25 "Communique," Church of God Executive Offices, Cleveland, Tenn., Feb. 23, 1970, p. 1.

26 *Mount Paran Messenger,* Mount Paran Church of God Bulletin (Feb. 18, 1970), Paul L. Walker, Pastor, Atlanta, Georgia, p. 1.

The global picture for the Pentecostal is much the same. In some countries the Pentecostal Movement is growing from nine to fifteen times as fast as the historical churches. Dr. John Mackay, president emeritus of Princeton Theological Seminary, announced that Protestantism is growing faster in Latin America than the population and the greatest gains have been made by the Pentecostals and other groups unrelated to the historic churches. *Time* magazine reported that Pentecostals outnumber traditional Protestants by at least four to one in most Latin countries. According to Dr. Eugene Nido, Secretary of the American Bible Society, the Pentecostals represent about eighty percent of all evangelical believers in Latin America. Dr. A. Marcus Ward has observed that the Pentecostals are growing too fast for any accurate statistics to be available.

It is reported that there are now three million Pentecostals in Indonesia, a half million in South Africa and five thousand in Oslo, Norway, alone. Field director of Greater Europe Mission, Royal L. Peck says, "One of the few bright spots in Italy has been the accomplishments of the Pentecostals. In the past forty years they have established seven hundred churches and now number one hundred thousand, or half of all Protestants in Italy."[27] The Pentecostal revival has been prominent in post World War II, Germany, with presently sixty thousand members. It is reported that there are between two hundred fifty thousand and three hundred thousand Pentecostal Christians in Russia. These are about half of all the Evangelicals. Romania, Yugoslavia, Poland and Hungary are significant for Pentecostal works, though they are

---

27 Royal L. Peck, "The Myth of Christian Italy," *World Vision Magazine* (May, 1966), p. 6.

frequently restricted. Even China has an estimated one hundred thousand Pentecostal believers.[28]

Prophetically, the eyes of the church-world are upon the Ecumenicals and the Pentecostals. In his General Assembly address in Dallas, Wade H. Horton stated, "God has raised up this Pentecostal movement for such a time as this. The eyes of all Protestantism are upon two groups, the Modernists and the Pentecostals. I believe this is our day."[29] A. W. Tozer stated it another way: "God may set aside so-called Evangelicals and raise up another movement to keep New Testament Christianity alive on the earth. Say not, 'We are children of Abraham.' God is able of these stones to raise up children unto Abraham."[30]

The historic nominal church has lost its voice of authority. Its trumpet gives forth uncertain sounds. It has lost its direction. Instead of pointing the way, it has fallen in the way. Instead of leading the crowd, it has followed the crowd. Like a traffic director suddenly gone blind, it is waving its hands in every direction. In the creation when the earth was without form and void and darkness was upon the face of the deep, the Spirit of God moved bringing beauty and order out of chaos. Our dilemma is similar in that it has prompted the contemporary move of the Spirit.

The church has not surrendered and it is far from running up the flag. The true Church will endure be-

28 Charles W. Conn, "Pentecost Around the World," *Church of God Evangel* (July 4, 1966). (Reprinted by permission from *Christian Life*), pp. 12, 13, 19.

29 Wade H. Horton, "Pentecost Yesterday and Today," Pathway Press, Cleveland, Tenn., 1964, pp. 109, 114.

30 A. W. Tozer, "Are They For Us Today?" *Christian Life*, October, 1957, p. 25.

cause of Pentecost. It will triumph because it is defined and supported by the irresistible power of the Holy Spirit. The Spirit has not withdrawn, but is ever present in the life and activity of Christ's body on this earth. Such assurance was given by a message in tongues and the interpretation which said, "If you will be the same to me as they (the apostles) were, I will be the same to you that I was to them" (Heb. 13:8).[31]

The Pentecostal ground swell has not been without its difficulties from without and within. As L. H. Aultman once stated, "With progress you have problems." In times of spiritual renewal and revolution, excesses and error are almost inevitable. As did Simon the Sorcerer (Acts 8:18, 19), some see the move of God as an opportunity for self-advantage. Discretion, wisdom and biblical instruction in love are necessary to protect any revival against error.

Periodically, one can expect new tags and trends to appear. It is like a new label on an old bottle, or the same product with a new advertising gimmick. The heretofore disinterested religious and secular press has brought some of this about by their sudden attention to the Pentecostal phenomenon. Such labels as the "spiritual renaissance," the "new penetration," "spiritual renewal," "neo-Pentecostalism" and others are constantly in the news. Contrary to the thinking of many, this is not a new revival. This twentieth century outpouring did not begin in 1956 or 1960. It is but an added surge of what has been enjoyed since the turn of the century.

One of the gravest abuses of a sacred term has been the mid-century uprising of groups called "Latter Rain."

---

31 Wade H. Horton, "Remembering A Pentecostal Phenomenon," *Church of God Evangel*, December 29, 1969, p. 3.

Down through the centuries this term has been used to describe revival (Deut. 11:14; Hosea 6:3; Joel 2:23; Zech. 10:1; James 5:7). The term was brought to much disrepute as maverick groups and individuals proclaimed a self-styled existence for the purpose of proselyting, confusing and plundering the organized Pentecostal churches. Some floated through the country, like an Elmer Gantry, preying upon anyone who would listen to their appeal. Others set up independent associations for the purpose of building family financial security. Infatuated by the flash of the moment, innocent people were soon left without a shepherd to lead them, a church to love them and a fellowship to comfort them. Embarrassed and confused, such were often ashamed to return to their scriptural churches from which they were enticed. Many have fallen by the way, never to regain their faith in God or in man. One by one, a few return to the church that still loves them and proves that love by longing and praying for their return.

These statements are not given to place a blanket of suspect over all independent individuals and groups, for there are some who selflessly give of their all to serve humankind with the gospel. It is given, however, to warn the innocent and the non-suspecting of recurring underground revolutionaries who periodically conjure up a closed view of "spirituality" and purport to have a corner on the spiritual market or a monopoly on God. Their attitude is highly critical of all except their own. They seem to be the only ones who know what real "spirituality" is and thus set themselves up as both judge and jury to every man and church. They know how everyone else ought to live, yet are exempt from the same standards which they impose upon others. They publicly and privately accuse others of not being "spiritual," yet their inconsistencies are some of the most carnal when examined by the Scriptures.

The reasons why some leave the church are often traced to a desire to hide or license a moral problem, to feed a gnawing ego or the greed for filthy lucre (Rom. 16:17, 18; 2 Tim. 4:10; Titus 1:11; 1 Peter 5:2; 3 John 9). The stock line and key phrase is the spectacular and the sensational. "Great things" are always happening with them and nothing is happening elsewhere. Fear, the mystical, pseudo-rewards, the power of suggestion, putting one on the spot, mob psychology, mass hypnosis and hysteria are used as motivational factors.

One is prompted to ask why this periodic gullibility for the spectacular and the sensational which often ends up in deception? Has our gospel appeal been misdirected? How many times do we have to get burned or tricked before we learn our lesson? Does this craving for the unreal mean that we are not satisfied with the real? Is the true spiritual man not satisfied with the real revelation of God as found in Jesus Christ and in the Scriptures? Why this longing for the way out, the new and the unheard of? What meaneth this "believer following signs" rather than "signs following believers"? If it is new, it is not necessarily true and neither is it necessarily false. The true test of spirituality is the test of the Scriptures, for the Spirit and the Word agree (1 John 4:1-6, 5:7, 8). This is illustrated by the Mother who told her daughter, "God said for you to leave your husband." Such a suggestion, however, is not borne out by the Scriptures (Matt. 19:5, 6, 9; 1 Cor. 7:10; 1 Peter 3:1). This is what often happens when so-called special revelation is used to replace the real revelation which is the Word of God.

Neo-Pentecostalism is a term that is used to define glossolalists who attend the historic churches. This new movement has spread rapidly throughout most nominal and traditional churches. It has its basis primarily in tongues' speaking. Groups and individuals are found in the Catholic, Episcopal, Lutheran, Presbyterian, Methodist, Baptist, Greek Orthodox and other denominations. They are also active in such universities, colleges and seminaries as Yale, Princeton, Notre Dame and Asbury. It is common today for a headline to read, "Speaking in Tongues Spreading to Most Denominations."[32] The *Baptist and Reflector* declared, "The New Pentecost is not limited to the Pentecostal sects. It has leaped all boundaries."[33] Some neo-Pentecostals do not wish to leave their existing churches in preference to a Pentecostal church. The traditional churches have been forced to adjust in order to retain these people. Some have made allowances, while others have excommunicated or barred those who speak in tongues.

With their widespread background and singular distinctive, many unconventional tendencies and teachings have arisen among the neo-Pentecostals. It is necessary that these be reviewed and assessed. Some of them are as follows: (1) that those who once speak in tongues can now do so at will; (2) that one should practice speaking in tongues often so as to enlarge his vocabulary; (3) that speaking in tongues is a psychological phenomenon which provides cathartic therapy for the release of tension; (4) that churches form Holy Spirit fellowships so as to confine speaking in tongues to closed

---

32 Tom Johnson, "Speaking in Tongues," *El Paso Times,* September 27, 1964, p. 9.
33 Clifford Ingle, "What About the New Pentecostalism?" *Baptist and Reflector,* November 10, 1966, p. 3.

sessions, thus avoiding the sanctuary; (5) that conversion is not a prerequisite to the infilling of the Spirit and speaking in tongues eliminates the basic aspect of salvation; (6) that one has no obligation to consider holiness or sanctification as a prerequisite to receiving the Holy Spirit, as holiness is leap-frogged direct to glossolalia; (7) that methods of receiving include: (a) by faith alone, (b) by repeating syllables and phrases as a preparatory exercise, (c) by deep breathing exercises thus inbreathing the Holy Spirit; (8) that the impartation and distribution of spiritual gifts are at the whim and discretion of man; (9) that the Spirit can be operated and the gifts exercised at will.

In accessing these trends it should be understood that these are not found among all neo-Pentecostals. Dr. Ray H. Hughes warns,

> One should use extreme caution with corrective measures concerning the things of the Spirit lest the wheat be uprooted with the tares. The term "Pentecostal" is so widely used until it now embraces practices and doctrines which true Pentecostals would never condone or endorse. Thus it behooves us to point up errors as a warning lest some stumble unnecessarily. . . . This is done with a deep concern for the continuation of this revival along scriptural lines. The equipment for world evangelism has been rediscovered and the opportunity must not be prostituted through error.[34]

Much of the misunderstanding and misrepresentation is brought about by taking the glossolalia phenomenon out of its scriptural place. A gift, endowment or blessing appropriated by the Scripture must of necessity be regulated and governed by the same authority. To speak in

---

34 Ray H. Hughes, "Glossolalia in Contemporary Times," *The Glossolalia Phenomenon*, Wade H. Horton, Editor, pp. 168, 169.

tongues at will, to disburse and use the gifts accordingly is to ignore the instructions of the Scripture. It is the Spirit that gives the utterance (Acts 2:4).* It is the Spirit that disburses the gifts "severally as he will" (1 Cor. 12:11). Man is not to use the Spirit but is to be used by the Spirit. The question as to who operates the gifts is positively answered in the Scriptures (1 Cor. 12:4-6, 11). The Spirit does not operate at the whim of man, but as He (the Holy Spirit) wills. Tongues are a purposeful sign and gift and are not to be manipulated according to the fancies of men nor to satisfy the curiosity of men. Gifts are not imparted by man, but by God, who according to His sovereign will distributes the gifts to whomsoever He desires.**

Prerequisites to the Holy Spirit baptism are clearly enunciated in the Scriptures. Paul asked, "Have ye received the Holy Ghost since ye believed?" This is still relevant today (Acts 19:2). The Holy Spirit baptism may be received at the time of conversion (subsequent to) as in the case of Paul and the Gentiles (Acts 9:17, 18, 10:43-48). It can also be received long after conversion as in the case of the disciples, the Samaritans and the Ephesians (Acts 2:1-11, 8:12-23, 19:1-7). Always conversion is involved as a prerequisite to receiving the infilling of the Holy Spirit. It is easy for some to fall into the error of ignoring the transformation of the born-again experience when they are encouraged to seek "glossolalia" rather than salvation. A Catholic priest testified in California that he was so pleased with the experience of speaking in tongues and that he might even try the new birth.

---

* See page 17 under "The Initial Evidence," especially footnote 52.
** For a further assessment read "Errors of the New Penetration," by Ray H. Hughes in *Glossolalia Phenomenon*, pp. 168-175.

Holiness was never intended to be a substitute for the baptism of the Holy Spirit and neither was the Spirit baptism intended to be a substitute for the sanctified life. Both experiences fill a definite need and follow a scriptural pattern. When reversed it is like trying to run dirty and unoiled machinery, building a hot fire with ashes, or ironing a starched garment that has never been washed. It might look all right at first glance, but you can see through it after awhile. To negate holiness and consign the Holy Spirit's power to the total end of glossolalia is to miss the real purpose of Pentecost. Any attempt to exercise glossolalia separate and apart from holiness is to invite carnality, disaster and shipwreck. The bodies of Christians are temples (1 Cor. 3:17). The reception of the Spirit is on the premise of a clean heart through repentance, faith and obedience (Acts 2: 38, 5:32, 15:8).

Methods of receiving the baptism of the Holy Spirit are also to be scripturally based. All things received of God are by faith and according to His grace. Faith alone without preparation for reception is not sufficient (1 Cor. 3:17, 6:19). Dr. Ray H. Hughes says, "The practice of repeating syllables as a preparatory exercise is totally unbiblical. To mouth certain syllables as a 'pump priming operation' is unnecessary. The Holy Spirit does not need this type of human intervention. The speaker in tongues speaks only as the Spirit gives utterance."[35] A misinterpretation of Psalm 81:10 and John 20:22 has prompted the practice of trying to inbreathe the Spirit. These Scriptures taken within their context do not mean that by breathing one can inhale the Spirit.

---

35 *Ibid.*, p. 171.

Physical breathing, whether inbreathing or outbreathing, has nothing to do with receiving the Holy Spirit.

Other dangers that trap neo-Pentecostals include the flare for the spectacular and a desire to "do your own thing," which often leads to "can you top this" sessions that glorify man rather than Christ. There is the subtle preoccupation with self rather than serving one's fellowman or his neighbor. There is also the danger of exalting the Spirit to a place above the Lord Jesus Christ, thus developing a new kind of Unitarianism. Historically, the overzealous are often divisive and abusive by their over-patronizing statements. Finally, there is always the danger of trying to force a stylized spiritual experience or a stereotyped mold of man upon others when the Holy Spirit is seeking to conform each believer into the likeness of Jesus Christ.[36]

It is obvious to all that there is a difference among Pentecostals. One of the great differences is a totally "experience centered" criterion with little or no regard for scriptural sanction or guidance. Every emphasis points purely to an "experience" of getting or to something super-ultra that happens to the individual. A. W. Tozer sensed the danger when he said,

> Certain brethren have magnified one gift out of seventeen beyond all proportion. Among these there have been many godly souls, but the general moral result has not been good. In practice, it has resulted in much shameless exhibitionism and a tendency to depend upon experiences instead of upon Christ, and often a lack of ability to distinguish the works of the flesh from the operation of the Spirit. Those who deny the gifts and those who make a hobby of the one are both

---

36 Russell T. Hitt, "The New Pentecostalism," *Eternity*, April, 1970, p. 13.

wrong and we are all suffering the consequences of their error.[37]

All seekers of truth loathe deception, for the Bible cautions, "Be not deceived" (1 Cor. 6:9, 15:33; Gal. 6:7). An experience is no guarantee against deception, neither is goodness or good works. W. E. Tull says,

> Truth is the only guarantee against deception. The only guarantee against a lie is the truth of God. An experience is not everything and every spiritual experience is not of God. God did not say to take a bad attitude toward such, but He did say to prove it (Matt. 7:16; 1 John 4:1; 2 Cor. 13:5). Some meat looks good but when examined is found to be rotten. Only God is willing to be proven (Mal. 3:10). The devil is not. The only weapon against deception is the Word of God. Christians should therefore put all things to the test of the Scriptures.[38]

No experience is beyond scriptural examination and evaluation. John says that we are to test the spirits (1 John 4:1). It is contrary to the New Testament for any person to remove his experience from the searchlight of the Scriptures. No experience can claim to be of God if the person having the experience refuses to validate it by the New Testament. If I am a New Testament Christian, it is my responsibility to test spirits for there are many spirits in the world (Rom. 12:2; Gal. 6:4). I would be derelict in my duty if I took all spiritual experiences at face value and did not test them according to the Word (1 Thess. 5:21). Christians must be willing to submit all that they believe, practice and experience to this test. The Spirit will give true experiences to those who seek

---

37 A. W. Tozer, "Are They for Us Today?" in *Christian Life*, October, 1957, p. 25.

38 W. E. Tull, Bible Study lecture notes, Dakota Camp Meeting, July, 1969.

according to the Word and He will reject that which is contrary and out of harmony with the Word.

James L. Slay says, "It is the function of the Bible to interpret experience, rather than experience to interpret the Scriptures."[39] The slope in the New Testament is from truth to experience, not from experience to truth. If one reverses the order, he does so at the expense of truth. While Christian experiences are indeed wonderful, they cannot be justified by this criterion alone. Experiences are real and valid because they conform to the Word of God and not because they are wonderful. The Holy Spirit never inspires any experience that is contrary to the New Testament, no matter how luminous or remarkable it may seem. The Christian who desires to have the most and best of the Holy Spirit must seek those things prescribed by the New Testament.

The role of the church in the present continuum is the same as the Early Church. As Paul would not allow the Corinthians to remove their experience from testing and instructions, but insisted that they conform to sound doctrine and proper church order, so must the church today. Bad experiences are always those whose scriptural basis is questionable and good experiences are those which rest upon the foundation of sound doctrine.

What would the contemporary church do without the Epistles? Paul knew the infant church was surrounded by wicked forces on the outside and harbored wolves on the inside (Acts 20:29). His only hope for their survival was "sound doctrine." It was his conviction that the hope of the church lay in its fidelity to Holy Scripture (2 Tim. 3:15-17). If Paul's opinions are correct,

---

39 James L. Slay, *This We Believe, op. cit.,* p. 64.

it is not going to be a revival of unusual spiritual experiences that saves the church and the world, but a return to the health and life-giving character of the Word. Ours must not be an "either, or" choice between dead orthodoxy or unruly unusual religious experiences. Ours must be a New Testament synthesis of truth that will inspire, shape and direct the church into a total experience of Christlikeness.[40]

Robert Morris, President of Yale University's Christian Fellowship, observed:

> We are little babies in this dimension of existence. We are very much in need of counsel and guidance lest we botch up the whole works.[41]

Assemblies of God General Superintendent Thomas F. Zimmerman places the responsibility squarely on the shoulders of the church.

> The Pentecostal Movement has a tremendous responsibility to the present day outpouring of the Holy Spirit that is everywhere apparent in the world today. Our responsibility centers around the areas of experience, example and exposition. We ought to be helping, training and informing the newcomers to Pentecost of some of the pitfalls and giving them the benefit of the lessons we have learned. We need to share what God has revealed to us concerning the gifts of the Spirit, their manifestations in the church, and the manner of receiving the baptism of the Holy Spirit. We ought to produce more books, pamphlets and study courses on the subject. . . . We who minister ought to take the initiative to be brotherly and meet interested min-

---

40 Bernard Ramm, "Hand In Hand," *His* Magazine, November, 1965, pp. 5-7.

41 "Holy Spirit Outpouring at Yale University," *Lighted Pathway*, Vol. 34, May 1963, p. 16.

isters and friends on the local level where we can
share with them what God has given us.[42]

The Church of God is a Pentecostal church which is
evangelistic, Christ centered, humanly oriented and Scripturally based. Because Jesus Christ, the living Word,
and the Bible, the written Word, are eternally contemporary, we are unafraid of examination, change and progress. We find strength in Bible definitions, experiences,
demonstrations and manifestations. We have applied the
relevancy of this truth to all walks of life and we are
witnessing its contemporaneity in a scientific space age.

The great tragedy of the modern historic church is that
the most dynamic force in the primitive Early Church is
missing—the power of the Holy Spirit. Whenever so-
called believers ignore, and in many cases fight the full
gospel emphasis on the Holy Spirit, they lose His power.
They cease to be active in witnessing for Christ. They
dry up spiritually and the Spirit is grieved. Without spiritual power, organized religion is like the dried-up bed of
a stream along which the waters once danced and sang,
but now they are drained away. It is not enough to believe in God. We must know Him as present and active
in our lives in the Person of His Spirit. The Holy Spirit
is not an experience alone, He is a Person. He is a
living power performing in us and through us the will
of God. If we are rich in goods but ragged in spirit,
then, to a crisis of the spirit we need the answer of the
Spirit.

---

42 Thomas F. Zimmerman, "The Pentecostal Movement's Responsibility
to the Present Day Outpouring," *The Pentecostal Evangel*, March 1, 1964,
pp. 2, 9.

Conclusion:

The Holy Spirit in You

"The promise is unto you . . . even as many as the Lord our God shall call" (Acts 2:39).

Jesus foresaw the crisis of the church and so He said, "It is expedient for you that I go away. . . . Tarry ye . . . until ye be endued with power from on high. . . . As the Father hath sent me, even so send I you. And when he had said this, he breathed on them, and saith unto them, Receive ye the Holy Ghost" (John 16:7, 20:21, 22; Luke 24:49). The baptism of the Holy Ghost is to be experienced. It is not merely a subject for formal thinking. The Holy Spirit baptism is not an optional extra. It is not in the category with those things that would be nice to have, but not really important if you do not have it. It is pointedly and specifically the will of God for every believer to be filled with the Spirit (Eph. 5:18). R. H. Gause says,

> The baptism of the Holy Spirit should never have become a denominational distinctive. It is not exclusive

139

> to Pentecostal churches for people to be filled with
> the Holy Spirit. Pentecost is Christianity and Chris-
> tianity is Pentecost.[1]

Whatever prerequisite you lack—seek it now. If you
need to be saved, then repent of your sins and accept
Jesus Christ as your Saviour (Acts 2:28). If you need to
be sanctified and set apart as a vessel to be used of
God, then tarry before Him for this purpose (John 17:15-
17, 23). If you need to be filled with the Spirit, pray
(Luke 11:13; Acts 1:14); and ask others to pray (Acts
8:15), believe (Matt. 21:22; Mark 11:24; Gal. 3:14)
and receive (John 14:15-17, 16:24, 20:21, 22). Remember that the Holy Spirit is a Gift and it is natural
for a gift to be received (Acts 10:45).

When John said, "Come . . . take the water of life
freely" (Rev. 22:17), he used the same word for "take"
as he used for "receive" in John 20:22. He referred to the
act of reaching out and taking a gift that is extended
by the Giver. This happens when the hand that is turned
downward is met by the hand turned upward. When
John spoke of Christ he said, "As many as *received* him,
to them gave he power to become the sons of God"
(John 1:12). God gives, but we must take the Gift from
the Giver. If you know how to receive Christ and how
to take the water of life freely, then you know how to
receive the baptism of the Holy Ghost. As P. F. Fritz
used to testify, "It's real, children! Go after it. Take ye
the Holy Ghost."[2]

The results of your personal Pentecost will be char-

---

1 R. H. Gause, *Convocation Lectures* (March 12, 1970), Northwest
Bible College, Minot, N. D.

2 Rev. P. F. Fritz, pioneer minister in the Church of God; the author
served as his pastor the last two years of his ninety-six year span.

acteristic of the Early Church. You, too, will receive power
for service to witness from "house to house," in the inner
city, in the suburbs, to the minorities and to those overseas (Acts 1:8). You, too, will continue steadfastly in
the Apostles' doctrine, in fellowship and in prayer (Acts
2:42). You, too, will become a regular worshiper—"con-
tinually in the temple" (Luke 24:53). And if not already,
you too, will become an involved church member, for they
added to the church daily "such as should be saved" (Acts
2:46, 47).

This power must never be limited to First Century
Christians alone. The baptism of the Holy Spirit is for
all believers. It is a definite part of the believer's inheri-
tance in Christ. The New Testament "all" gives evidence
that the Early Church believed the Spirit baptism to be
a normative experience for every believer (Acts 2:4,
4:31, 10:44). There is no valid reason why all believers
should not be filled with the Spirit, for the Holy Spirit
is a divine Gift to be imparted to all who ask for Him
(Luke 11:13).

With the imminent return of Christ upon us, all believers should look up and receive the promise (Acts
2:39).

> Hover o'er me, Holy Spirit,
> Bathe my trembling heart and brow;
> Fill me with thy hallowed presence,
> Come, O come and fill me now.

142

INSTRUCTIONS FOR PREPARING A WRITTEN REVIEW

1. A certificate of credit will be awarded when the student satisfies the requirements listed on page 6.

2. The student, at a time designated by the instructor, should write the missing words in the sentences below on a blank sheet of paper and present it to the instructor for processing.

3. In the case of home study, the student should present his answers to the pastor or someone whom he may designate.

A CONTEMPORARY STUDY OF THE HOLY SPIRIT

by Bennie S. Triplett

CTC 305—Written Review

1. The word "Holy" is used in the Scriptures to refer to persons and things which are sacred and set apart for _____ uses.

2. The Spirit is called "Holy" because He is the spirit of the Holy One, and His _____ work is sanctification.

3. The first great schism in the modern _____ churches took place because of the so-called New Light—New Issue—"Jesus Only" Doctrine, those who baptize in "Jesus Name" and feel that a person is not really converted unless one believes as they do and are baptized as they are.

4. When Pentecostals use the word "baptism" referring to the Holy Ghost, they are referring to the historic moment when the individual was _____ filled with the Spirit.

5. Article nine of the Church of God Declaration of Faith states "We believe . . . in speaking with other tongues as the Spirit gives utterance, and that it is the _____ evidence of the baptism of the Holy Ghost.

6. Speaking in tongues is the _____ phrase which scholars term glossolalia.

7. Primarily, Pentecostals do not magnify glossolalia, but rather the _____ benefits of the baptism with the Holy Ghost.

8. The Holy Ghost Himself is the power, when you have Him you have all the _____ you need to do anything God wants you to do.

9. The function of the Holy Spirit is to fill a man with that which would make him able _____ to cope with life.
10. In the _____ Church, Pentecost is the anniversary of the coming of the Holy Spirit.
11. The oldest _____ church in America is the Church of God.
12. When God's Spirit gave us the Bible, He gave us the only _____ guidebook.
13. A new understanding of sin will bring a _____ conviction about righteousness.
14. True conversion will involve the _____ being.
15. There is only one answer for a sin-sick world and that is a _____ life for the individual wrought by the regenerating power of the Holy Spirit.
16. The _____ student of the Holy Spirit should be able to distinguish between the numerous baptisms mentioned in the Scripture.
17. Witnessing for Christ is the _____ obligation of all Christians.
18. The direction of our witness is "_____ in Jerusalem, and all Judea, and in Samaria, and unto the uttermost part of the earth."
19. Ray H. Hughes says, "All of the _____ gifts are resident in the Holy Ghost, and when one is full of the Holy Ghost, he has the potential of all the spiritual gifts."
20. Donald Gee says, "The Word of Wisdom is the teaching of the _____ things of God which the Spirit alone can search out and reveal."
21. The Church of God believes that _____ healing is provided for all in the Atonement.
22. A true prophet is a man with a message from God who interprets His divine will and purpose in _____ preaching and teaching.
23. The gift of discernment should be distinguished from _____ skills which understand and predict human behavior.
24. The chief end of the charismata is to build up, promote _____ growth and to develop character.
25. Spiritual gifts are _____ for demonstrating love.
26. A _____ balanced Christian is a blessing wherever he goes.
27. The disuse of the gifts can be traced to our failure in teaching their _____ use.
28. The exercise of all the gifts should be the _____ thing in all churches and should bring honor only to God.
29. The flesh refers to _____ nature as weakened and tainted by sin; man, as he is apart from Jesus Christ and His Spirit.
30. The Christian _____ is a completely harmonized and unified life with Christ at the center.
31. It is no accident that the Bible places _____ emphasis on love.

32. The _____ common New Testament word for love is "agape."

33. The Cross means that God has reached _____ to us that we might reach out to others.

34. The believer's joy begins with his acceptance of Jesus as Saviour and it continues to be the atmosphere of his _____ _____ life.

35. In the New Testament the principle meaning of peace (eirene) is "salvation"—the salvation of the _____ man—complete reconciliation with God.

36. Christians, however, are concerned with _____ peace which is both inward and outward.

37. Perserverence is that _____ patience by which the Christian contends against the hindrances, persecutions and temptations of the inside and outside world.

38. Christ is our ideal _____ and pattern of goodness.

39. Meekness is probably the most unpopular and misunderstood of all _____ virtues.

40. When the Holy Spirit is at the controls, all _____ of life will be brought under the Lordship of Jesus Christ.

41. The Spirit produces His _____ fruit as we trust and cooperate.

42. Fewer than one-third of the world's inhabitants are now identified with Christendom, and Christians are being outpaced by population _____ and revivals in other religions.

43. Traditions that are not founded upon the Scriptures are judged as the traditions of men which are often _____ in competition with and in opposition to the commandments of God.

44. Evangelicalism is founded upon the _____ basic principles of fundamentalism; namely, the inerrancy of the Scriptures, the virgin birth, the substitutionary atonement, the physical resurrection and the imminent physical return of the Lord Jesus Christ.

45. The _____ voice of the Church of God is its General Assembly composed of both ministry and laity.

46. More than an "anti-movement" against something Protestantism is a protest for _____ Christianity.

47. One of the _____ abuses of a sacred term has been the mid-century uprising of groups called "Latter Rain."

48. Tongues are a _____ sign and gift and are not to be manipulated according to the fancies of men nor to satisfy the curiosity of men.

49. The Spirit will give _____ experiences to those who seek according to the Word and He will reject that which is contrary and out of harmony with the Word.

50. The New Testament "all" gives evidence that the _____ _____ church believed the Spirit baptism to be a normative experience for every believer.